Excel

For Everyone

2022

A Guide that teaches you to use excel from beginner to advanced level comprehensive of examples and tips

BY STUART STOKES

TABLE OF CONTENT

CHAPTER 6: PIVOT TABLES IN EXCEL — 91

CHAPTER 7: CONDITIONAL FORMATTING IN EXCEL — 116

CHAPTER 8: CELL REFERENCING 126

CHAPTER 9: TIPS AND TRICKS 135

CHAPTER 10: FAQS 154

INTRODUCTION

MS Excel is a worksheet software created in 1985 by the Microsoft Company. It is a frequent spreadsheet methodology that handles data in rows & columns that might be controlled using formulas that enable the application to do statistical calculations on the data.

Thanks to its ability to adjust to nearly every business method, Excel is plausibly the extremely easy, scalable, & commonly used business form around the globe at the moment. After utilized in combination with other Microsoft Office applications such as Outlook, MS Word, & MS PowerPoint, there is a very small possibility that this potent combination might not handle it.

With the net playing such a vital role in our businesses, it is just natural that the interests of the several would win out. Continuing present on latest technology has come to be a full-time task as Microsoft applications keep growing. MS Excel shall continue to be the top popular software for assessing data, creating presentations & charts, & combining with practical tools for graphical interfaces & business communication plans.

Businesses are gradually switching to cloud computing for data accessibility and collaboration. In the later years, you see

Excel's future pressing at a quick speed to approach multi-user access to immense data for reporting, study, & major enhancements in productivity & result.

Custom outcomes are required in today's strong market ambiance to keep an economical benefit & maximize profit. Excel is arguing firms are the most skilled considering existing & evolving technologies. Getting a maintained expert adviser is vital to achieving the full power & increased productivity essential to be productive in this twenty-first century. For MS Excel results & guidance, you are recommended to make contact with them at present.

Chapter 1:

Introduction to MS Excel 2021

1.1 What Does MS Excel Mean?

MS Excel is a software application formed by Microsoft that lets users manage, format, & calculate data with formulas using a spreadsheet system.

This software is part of the Microsoft Office suite and is compatible with other applications in the Office suite. Like other MS Office products, MS Excel could now be acquired through the cloud on a payment basis across Office 365.

MS Excel is indeed a commercial spreadsheet tool developed by Microsoft and published for the Microsoft Windows & Mac OS operating systems. It includes, among other things, the ability to make simple calculations, use graphical tools, construct pivot tables, and create macros.

To organize and manage data, a spreadsheet programmer like MS Excel employs a collection of cells organized into rows and columns. They could also use line graphs, histograms, and charts to present data.

MS Excel allows users to organize information to see various elements from multiple angles. Visual Basic is a language of programming that may be used to develop a range of advanced numerical algorithms in Excel. Programmers have the option of creating code directly in Visual Basic Editor, which includes Windows for debugging & organizing code modules.

History & Future of MS Excel

Excel played a critical role in bookkeeping & record-keeping for business operations in the early stages of available PC business computing.

A table with just an auto sum format is one of the greatest examples of an MS Excel use case.

Entering a column of data and clicking into a cell at bottom of a spreadsheet, then using the "auto sum" button to enable that cell to add up all the numbers input above, is fairly simple with Microsoft Excel. This substitutes manual ledger totals, which remained a time-consuming element of business earlier to the progress of the contemporary worksheet.

MS Excel has come to be a must-have for several types of "business computing", including looking at regular, quarterly, or monthly data, organizing the payroll & taxes, & other

comparable business methods, thanks to the auto sum & other developments.

Microsoft Excel has become a crucial end-user technology, valuable in training & professional development, thanks to a variety of easy application cases. Microsoft Excel was included in the basic business diploma on business computers for a number of years, & temporary job agencies may assess persons for a variety of clerical roles based on their proficiency with MS Word and Microsoft Excel.

Microsoft Excel, on the other hand, has become largely outmoded in certain areas as business technology has progressed. This is due to a notion known as "visual dashboard" technology, often known as "data visualization."

In general, businesses and providers have devised innovative new ways to graphically show data that do not need end-users to examine a standard spreadsheet containing columns of numbers & IDs. Instead, they use graphs, charts, and other complex displays to better grasp and comprehend the statistics. People have recognized that "reading" a visual presentation is much easier.

The application cases for MS Excel have been altered as a result of the data visualization concept. Whereas in the past, organizations would have used MS Excel to manage hundreds of entries, today's commercial use cases often employ spreadsheets that handle only a few dozen data for each project.

If the spreadsheet has more than a few dozen rows, the information will be more efficient shown on a visual dashboard than in a standard spreadsheet style.

1.2 Why Should I Learn Microsoft Excel?

We all effort with statistics in some space. We all have ordinary costs that we recompence for with our weekly earnings. To devote properly, one must first understand their income and spending. When we want to capture, assess, & save numeric data, MS Excel comes in helpful. Let's look at an example utilizing the image below.

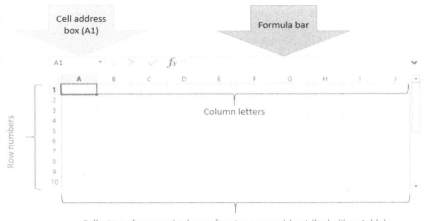

Where can I get Microsoft Excel?

Microsoft Excel is accessible in a variety of layouts. It is available from a laptop hardware shop that also deals in software. Microsoft Excel is an application that is part of the MS Office suite. You may also get it through the Microsoft website, but you'll have to pay for the license key.

1.3 How to Open Microsoft Excel?

Excel may be run in the same way as any other Windows software. Follow the steps below if you're using Windows with a graphical user interface:

- Select Start from the drop-down option.

- All programs should be pointed.

- Select Microsoft Excel.

If it's been added to the start menu, you may also launch it from there. If you've made a desktop shortcut, you may also use it to open it.

1.4 Understanding the Ribbon

In Excel, the ribbon gives shortcuts to commands. A command is indeed an action taken by the user. Making a different document, printing a file, & so on are instances of commands. The ribbon of Excel is seen in the image below.

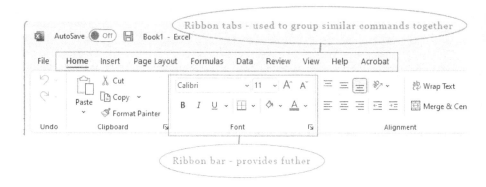

Ribbon components explained

A ribbon start icon is used to access functions such as making new files, printing, saving existing work, & accessing Excel customization choices, as well as others.

Ribbon tabs - the tabs are being used to organize instructions that are similar. Basic actions like formatting data to make it more attractive, sorting, and locating specific data inside the spreadsheet are performed on the main tab.

Ribbon bar - the bars are being used to organize instructions that are similar. The Alignment ribbon bar, for example, is used to organize all of the commands that are needed to align data altogether.

1.5 Understanding the worksheet

A worksheet is a set of columns and rows. A cell is formed when a row & a column meet. Data is recorded in cells. A cell address is used to identify each cell individually. Letters are used to mark columns, whereas numbers are used to label rows.

A set of worksheets is referred to as a workbook. A workbook in Excel has three cells by default. To meet your needs, you can delete/add more sheets. Sheet1, Sheet2, and so on are the default names for the sheets. You may rename the sheets to something more useful, like Daily Expenses or Monthly Budget, for example.

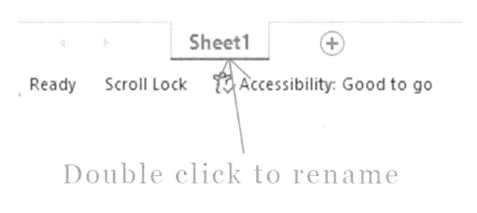

Double click to rename

1.6 Customization MS Excel Environment

It is preferred to be the color black because the MS Excel theme is blackish. If blue is your favorite color, you may make your theme color seem blue as well. You don't want to include ribbons tab such as developer if you are not a coder. All of this is possible thanks to modifications.

- Customization of the ribbon
- Settings for formulas
- Proofing settings
- Setting the color theme
- Save settings

Customization of ribbon

The default ribbons in Excel 2021 are seen in the image above. Let's start with the ribbon modification. Let's say you don't want to view any of the tabs on the ribbon, or you want to add some missing tabs, such as the developer tab. You may accomplish this by using the settings window.

- To begin, click the ribbon's file button.
- You must be able to see a dialogue box called Options in the bottom-left part of the interface.

- As illustrated below, select the customized ribbon option from the left-hand side panel.

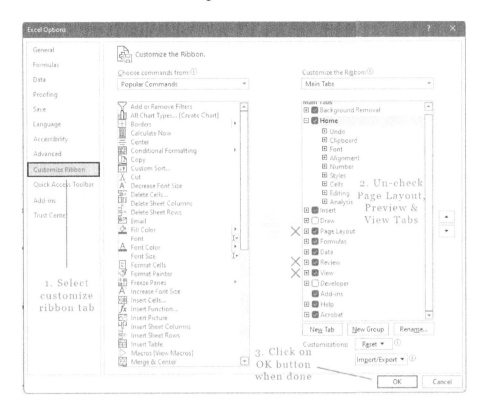

- Remove checkmarks from tabs on your right-hand side that you don't want to see on the ribbon. We've eliminated the Page Layout, Review, & View tabs for this example.

- When you're finished, click the "OK" button.

This is how your ribbon will appear.

Adding custom tabs to the ribbon

You may also create your own tab, name it whatever you like, and assign it instructions. Let's make a tab with the words Guru99 in the ribbon.

- Select Customize Ribbon from the context menu when you right-click on the ribbon. A dialogue window similar to the one seen above will display.

- As shown in the animated figure below, click the new tab button.

- Choose the newly added tab.

- Rename the file by clicking the Rename button.

- Give it the moniker Guru99.

- As illustrated in the figure below, go to the Guru99 tab and choose New Group (Custom).

- Give it a new name by clicking the Rename button. My Instructions

- Let's go ahead and add some instructions to my ribbon bar.

- On the middle panel, you'll find a list of commands.

- Select the command All chart types and then click the Add button.

- Select OK.

Your ribbon will look as follows

Setting the color theme

To change the color theme of an Excel sheet, go to the Excel ribbon and select the File Option. It will open the window where you must complete the tasks below.

1. By default, the general tab on the left-hand panel would be chosen.

2. Look under General settings for working with Excel for a color scheme.

3. Select the preferred color from the color scheme drop-down list.

4. Select the OK button.

Settings for formulas

You may use this option to control how Excel behaves while dealing with formulae. It may be used to configure settings such as autocomplete when inputting formulae, changing the cell referencing style, and using numbers for both columns & rows, among other things.

To make an option active, tick the box next to it. Remove the checkmark from the checkbox to disable an option. This option is available in the Options dialogue box, beneath the Formulas tab on the left-hand side panel.

Proofing settings

This option alters the text that has been typed into Excel. It allows you to customize things like the dictionary language which should be used when checking for misspellings, dictionary suggestions, and so on. This option is available in the settings dialogue box on the left-hand side panel, under the proofreading tab.

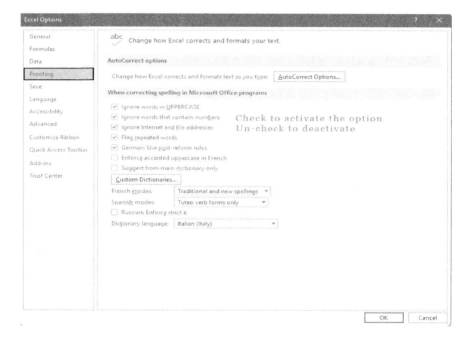

Save settings

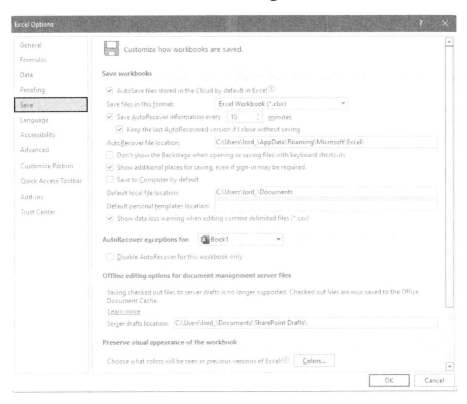

This option allows the user to set the default file format for saving files, as well as enable auto-recovery if your computer shuts down before you can save your work. This option is available in the Options dialogue box, under the Save tab on the left-hand side panel.

1.7 Best Practices when working with Microsoft Excel

- Workbooks should be saved with older systems in mind. You should save your files in 2003 .xls format for reusability if you are not using the latest capabilities in higher versions of Excel.

- In a workbook, give columns and worksheets descriptive names.

- Avoid working with formulae that include a lot of variables. Instead of constructing your own formulae, try breaking things down into little manageable outcomes that you can build on. Use built-in methods whenever possible.

CHAPTER 2:

EXCEL INTERFACE

2.1 File Tab & Ribbon

The Office button  has been replaced in Excel 2010 by a tweak to the traditional File menu. Click to show the options for New, Open, Save, Print, and Close.

If you're updating from 2007, you'll see that the UI hasn't changed much. If you're upgrading from an earlier version of Excel, however, you might be unaware of the new design, which will be detailed in the parts below. The top-left corner of the window is divided into seven tabs. When you click on a tab, a no. of alternatives will appear as buttons alongside text names and graphic icons to help you identify them. The Ribbon refers to the tabs & their possibilities. The choices are grouped into groups of relevant characteristics beneath the tabs. By clicking this arrow to the right of a group box, you may expand the groupings.

2.2 Home Tab

The Home tab in Excel offers the most often used text editing tools.

Shortcut Menu

The shortcut menu allows you to rapidly access the most often used Excel commands and functions. To use this feature, right-click or control-click the element you want to edit on a PC or regulate the element you want to edit on a Mac. Depending on the aspect you've chosen, the alternatives presented will change.

2.3 Spreadsheet Basics

Every MS Excel file is a workbook, and each workbook can include several worksheets. The worksheet consists of a grid of columns (denoted by letters) & rows (denoted by numbers) (designated by numbers). The blue buttons at the top of the worksheet identify the letters of columns. The row numbers are given by the blue buttons on the worksheet's left side. A cell is the point where a column & a row meet. You can fill in the blanks with your information. Text, numbers, and algorithms for automatic computations can all be entered into cells. The

cell address for each cell in the spreadsheet is indeed the column letter followed by row number.

Formula bar

As you use Excel, this will be one of the most useful tools. The formula bar displays all the details and procedures that were utilized to return the contents of a cell. When you enter data into the cell, the outputs, or final results, are displayed when you walk away from the cell. This is particularly obvious when using functions because you only see the answer of the equation inside the cell in a spreadsheet, not the whole equation. The formula bar remains below the ribbon & takes up much of the window.

Although hiding the formula bar is feasible, it is not advised. Go to the Excel Options at the bottom right of a menu that appears when you click the Office button to conceal or display the formula bar if it has been hidden by accident. To see the formula bar, go to the Advanced option & select the box for the Display formula bar under Display. Simply click Ok when you're finished.

Adding a Worksheet

Each Excel workbook comes with three worksheets by default. By clicking on the worksheet tabs above the status bar, you may access the various worksheets. Click on the Insert Worksheet tab to the right of the current worksheet tabs to create a new worksheet.

2.4 Renaming a Worksheet

To rename the worksheet tab, use one of the following methods:

Steps:

Option 1:

- If you're using a PC, right-click the tab you want to rename; if you're using a Mac, control-click the tab you want to rename. A choice of shortcuts will appear.

- From the shortcut menu, select Rename.

- Fill in the new name.

- Press the button.

Option 2:

- Double-click the tab you wish to rename after hovering over it.

- To rename the tab, start typing.

- Press the button.

2.5 Modifying a Worksheet

Add data to a cell, navigate among cells; add rows & columns to a spreadsheet. cut, copy, and paste cells. & resize columns & rows are all covered in this section. It also demonstrates how to utilize the freeze pane's function, which enables you to freeze column and row titles to make navigating a huge spreadsheet easier.

Adding Data to a Cell

To enter data into a cell, click it with your mouse and start typing.

Moving Through Cells

Use the keyboard instructions given below to go through the worksheet cells.

Movement Action	Key Combination
One cell up	up arrow key or +
One cell down	down arrow key or key
One cell left	left arrow key or +
One cell right	right arrow key or key
Top of the worksheet (cell A1)	+
End of the worksheet (last cell containing data)	<Ctrl< +
End of the row	+ right arrow key
End of the column	+ down arrow key

Moving to a Specific Cell:

To move to the specific cell:

Steps:

- In the Name Box, type your mobile phone number (cell letter first, then phone number).

	A	B	C	D	E	F	G
			C5 ∨ ⋮ ✕ ✓ fx 64				
	A	B	C	D	E	F	
1	Student	Midterm1	Midterm2	Paper	Final	Total Score	
2	Michael	25	90	10	91	216	
3	Tara	39	91	10	93	233	
4	Clare	95	87	9	89	280	
5	Sarah	76	64	10	90	240	
6	Henry	65	73	10	64	212	
7	Kim	78	90	10	86	264	
8	Jennifer	79	83	8	79	249	
9	Walter	85	62	10	93	250	
10							

- Press **Enter**

Adding a Row

A row is a horizontal line that goes across a spreadsheet. To add a row to a worksheet, do the following:

Steps:

- Select the worksheet on which you want the row to display.
- Go to the Home tab and choose it.
- In the Cells group, click the down arrow on the Insert button.
- Select Insert Sheet Rows from the drop-down menu.

Note: This will add a row to the right of the currently selected cell.

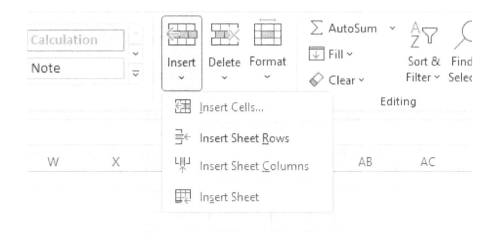

Adding a Column

A column is a horizontal row that goes vertically along with a worksheet. To add a column, follow these steps:

Steps:

- Select the worksheet on which you want the column to display.

- Go to the Home tab and choose it.

- In the Cells group, click the arrow on the Insert button.

- Select Insert Sheet Columns from the drop-down menu.

Note: By doing so, a column will be added to the left of the presently selected cell.

Shortcut Menu

To use the shortcut menu to insert rows or columns, type:

- To add a new row or column, click the row number/column letter where you want it to appear.

- If you're using a PC, right-click the column letter/row no; if you're using a Mac, control-click the column letter/row no. A choice of shortcuts will appear.

- From the shortcut menu, select Insert.

Note for rows: This will place the row above the one you've chosen.

Note for columns: This will move the column to the left of the one you've chosen.

Resizing a Column

To resize a column, do the following:

- To pick a worksheet, click anywhere on it.

- Hold your cursor over the column heading's edge until it transforms to a + sign.

- Click & drag until you're satisfied with the column's width.

Select the column headers you wish to edit, then click & drag one of the columns to the appropriate width.

Resizing a Row

To resize a row, do the following:

- To pick a worksheet, click anywhere on it.

- Hold your cursor over the row heading's boundary until it transforms to a plus symbol.

- Drag the width of the row until you're comfortable with it.

Select any row headings you wish to edit, then click & drag one of the rows to the appropriate width.

Selecting a Cell

You must first choose a cell before you can alter or format it. The table below shows you how to choose cells quickly.

Cells to Select	Mouse Action
One cell	Click once in the cell
Entire row	Click the row heading
Entire column	Click the column heading
Entire worksheet	Click the **Select All** button located above the row headings and to the left of the column headings, or press **Ctrl + A** on your keyboard.
Cluster of cells	Click and drag the mouse over the cell cluster

Cutting, Copying, & Pasting Cells

To transfer cells from one area on a worksheet to another, either cut/copy the cell(s), then paste cell(s) in their new location.

To cut a cell:

- To choose a cell, click it.

- Go to the Home tab and choose it.

- Press Ctrl + X on the keyboard or click the Cut button in the Clipboard group.

A blinking dotted border will now surround the cell.

To copy a cell:

- To choose a cell, click it.

- Go to the Home tab and choose it.

- Ctrl + C on the keyboard, or click the Copy button in the Clipboard group.

A blinking dotted border will now surround the cell.

To paste a cut/copied cell to a different spot on your worksheet, follow these steps:

- To pick a new position on your worksheet, click it.

- Go to the Home tab and choose it.

- Press Ctrl + V on the keyboard or click the Paste button in the Clipboard group.

If you're merely moving the contents of a single cell a short distance, the drag-& drop approach may be more convenient.

Steps:

- Select the cell you wish to move by clicking it. The cell's boundaries will be surrounded by a black border.

- Drag the cell to its new place by clicking and dragging its dark border.

Keeping Headings Visible

If you have a huge spreadsheet with a lot of column & row headings, they will disappear as you scroll down. You may utilize the Freeze Panes option if you want the headers to be always displayed. Separately freezing the column & row titles is required.

To keep the row headers frozen, do the following:

Steps:

- On the left side of the page, click the Row 1 heading.

- Toggle to the View tab.

- From a Window group, select the Freeze Panes icon.

- Freeze the top row by clicking the button.

To freeze the column headings:

- On the top of the spreadsheet, click the Column A heading.

- Toggle to the View tab icon.

- From a Window group, select the Freeze Panes icon.

- Freeze the first column by clicking the button.

To unfreeze a row, go to the View tab and click the Freeze Panes icon, then Unfreeze it.

2.6 Formatting Cells

From the Format Cells dialogue box, you may access formatting settings for cells. Do one of the following to bring up the Format Cells dialogue box.

- Choose the cell that has to be formatted. Right-click the cell on a PC. Users using Macs need to hold down Control & click the cell. Select Format Cells from the shortcut menu.

- Click the arrow in the Number group on the Home tab.

Formatting cells is done via the Format Cells dialogue box, which provides the following options:

- Number tab –allows you to choose a numerical data type, such as currency, Date, or percentage.

- Alignment tab –allows you to rearrange the data in a cell's location and alignment.

- Font tab – allows you to alter cell font properties such as font face, size, style, & color.

- Border –allows you to choose from a number of various border styles for your cell.

- Fill –allows you to shade and color the backdrop of a cell.

- Protection – You may use this feature to lock or hide a cell.

Dates and Times

Excel enters days in a spreadsheet in the format 1-Jan-01 by default. Excel will automatically detect the text as a date and transform it to "1-Jan-01" even if you enter the Date as «January 1, 2001.» If you want to use an alternate date format, type:

Steps:

- Select the cell to which you wish to apply the new date format.
- Go to the Home tab and choose it.
- Click Format in the Cells group.
- Select Format Cells from the Format menu. This will bring up the Format Cells dialogue box.
- Toggle to the Number tab.
- Select Date from the Category drop-down menu.
- From the drop-down menu, select the date format you desire.
- Click the OK button.

In addition, Excel inserts times in a specified way. If you want to use a variable time format, repeat the instructions above but change the Category menu to Time.

Styles

Excel has a variety of pre-defined styles that you may use to format your spreadsheet quickly and efficiently. The styles also contribute to a professional and uniform appearance for your spreadsheet.

To apply a preset design to a cell or a group of cells in your worksheet, follow these steps:

Steps:

- To choose a cell, click it.

- Go to the Home tab and choose it.

- Format as Table may be found in the Styles category. A menu appears, displaying the various cell styles. Hold the cursor over the menu choice to see a preview of a style.

- By clicking on a style, you may select it.

To add a preset style to the entire worksheet:

- By using CTRL + A on the keyboard, you may select all of the cells in your worksheet.

- Go to the Home tab and choose it.

- Format as Table may be found in the Styles category. A menu appears, displaying the formatting options available. Hold your mouse over a menu choice to see a sample of a style.

- By clicking on a style, you may select it.

Format Painter

If you've prepared a cell with a specific font style, border, date format, or other formatting settings, you can use the Format Painter tool to format a cell or group of cells in the same way.

Steps:

- To copy a format, place your cursor within the cell that contains the format you wish to duplicate.

- Select Format Painter from the Home menu. Your cursor will be accompanied by a paintbrush.

- Choose the cells you wish to format from the drop-down menu.

Double-click the Format Painter button to copy formatting to several groups of cells. Until you push the key, the format painter will stay active.

2.7 Formulas and Functions

One of the most useful features of the Excel spreadsheet application is the ability to design formulae that compute results automatically. A spreadsheet is nothing more than a huge table for showing text without formulae.

Formulas

A formula is a mathematical expression that performs computations depending on the information in your spreadsheet. In your worksheet, formulas are typed into a cell. They must start with an equal sign, then addresses of the cells which will be computed on, followed by a suitable operand. The computation begins as soon as the formula is input into the cell. In the formula bar, the formula appears.

A formula has been constructed for computing the subtotal of a lot of textbooks in the example below. This formula multiplies each textbook's quantity and price, then adds totals to get the total cost of all volumes.

| C7 | | ∨ | ⋮ | ✕ | ✓ | *fx* | =((B2*C2)+(B3*C3)+(B4*C4)+(B5*C5)) |

	A	B	C	D	E	F
1	Textbook	Quantity	Price			
2	Biology	4	$ 99,99			
3	Chemistry	2	$ 79,95			
4	Calculus	7	$ 65,99			
5	English	12	$ 49,99			
6						
7		Subtotal	$ 1.621,67			
8						

Linking Worksheets

You may utilize data from two distinct spreadsheets to generate a formula. This may be done either within a single worksheet or across many workbooks. When connecting cells from worksheets inside the same workbook, the base formula is represented as "sheet name.celladdress." When connecting cells from separate workbooks, the underlying formula is expressed as "[workbook-name.xlsx]sheetname.cell address." The formula "=A1+Sheet2. A2" may be used to add the values of cell A1 in Worksheet 1 & cell A2 in Worksheet 2. If Worksheet 1 is in Book1.xlsx and Worksheet 2 is in Book2.xlsx, the identical cells may be inserted using the formula "=[Book1.xlsx]Sheet1.$A$1+A2". Of course, this formula would be placed on Sheet 2 of Book2.xlsx.

Relative, Absolute, & Mixed Referencing

The technique of referring to cells just by their column & row names (such as "A1") is known as relative referencing. Excel does not make an exact copy of a formula that involves relative referencing and is transferred from one cell to another. Cell addresses will be changed about the row & column they are relocated to. If the basic addition formula "=(A1+B1)" in cell C1 is transferred to cell C2, the formula will change to "=(A2+B2)" to reflect the new row.

To avoid this, cells must be referenced using absolute referencing. This is performed by using the dollar signs "$" in the formula's cell addresses. Continuing with the preceding example, if cell C1's formula is "=($A$1+$B$1)," cell C2's value will equal the sum of cells A1 & B1. Both cells' columns and rows are absolute, meaning they will not alter when copied. When the row OR column is constant, but not both, mixed referencing can be utilized. In the formula "=(A$1+$B2)," for example, the row of cell A1 & the column of cell B2 are both fixed.

Basic Functions

When compared to formulae, functions could be a more efficient approach to conduct mathematical operations. You would use the formula "=D1+D2+D3+D4+D5+D6+D7+D8+D9+D10" if you wished to

sum the numbers of cells D1 through D10 or the sum function & enter "= SUM(D1:D10)" for a faster solution. In the table below, you'll find a number of different function instructions and examples:

The Function Wizard

Using the Function Wizard, you may access menus of various accessible functions in Excel. To use it to choose a function, follow these steps:

- Select the cell where you want the function to go.

- Select the Formulas tab from the Function Library group. The dialogue box for inserting a function appears.

Note: The identical Insert Function button is always located to the left of the Formula Bar & to the right of the Name Box.

Steps:

- Select a function category from the Category drop-down menu.

- Choose a function type from Select a function option. Below the menu, you'll find a description and an example of the function.

- Click the OK button. The dialogue window for Function Arguments appears.

- Select the cells which will be used to perform the function.

- Click OK once you've input all of the function's cell values.

Autosum

To add contents of a group of neighboring cells, use the Autosum function.

Steps:

- The group of cells which will be summed should be highlighted (cells B2 through G2 in this particular example).

- Navigate to the Formulas tab.

- Select Autosum from the menu Σ.

	Undo	Clipboard		Font				Styles

SUM		: $\times$ $\checkmark$ fx	=SUM B2:G2				

	A	B	C	D	E	F	G	H
1	M&M	Brown	Red	Orange	Yellow	Green	Blue	Total
2	Package 1	18	16	3	13	3	4	B2:G2
3	Package 2	22	9	5	10	6	6	
4	Package 3	12	13	6	10	6	11	
5	Package 4	17	10	7	10	10	3	
6	Package 5	15	7	10	16	6	5	
7								

2.8 Sorting & Filling

Sorting Data

After you've done putting data into the spreadsheet, you might want to arrange it to make it simpler to browse and search. You can, for example, place a list of the names in alphabetically or numerically order number entries. In a column, you may sort data in ascending/descending order.

To sort information in a column, do the following:

Steps:

- By choosing the column letter, you may choose the column you wish to sort.

- Go to the Home tab and choose it.

- From the Editing group, select the Sort and Filter option.

- If you want to sort the data in the ascending order, click $\overset{A}{Z}\downarrow$, or if you want it in descending order, click $\overset{Z}{A}\downarrow$.

Complex Sorts

It's possible that you'll have to sort your information by more than a column. If your undergraduate class has been allocated team projects, for example, you may have a column for project titles and a column for student names, as seen below.

You may sort all of the student names into project groups first, then alphabetize the student names inside each project group. To sort by several columns, use the following formula:

Steps:

- Select all the columns you'd want to sort.

- Go to the Home tab and choose it.

- Click Sort & Filter in the Editing group.

- Then choose Custom Sort. The Sort dialogue box appears on the screen.

- Select the first column to sort from the Column dropdown menu.

- Select A to Z from the Order dropdown menu to sort in the ascending order, or Z to A to sort in the descending order from Order dropdown menu.

- For the columns (remaining) you wish to sort, you'll need to create additional levels. By clicking Add Level button and selecting a level from Then by dropdown menu, you may create a new level.

- For each of the columns you wish to sort, enter the columns & values.

- Click the OK button.

Autofill

You may use the Autofill tool to quickly fill fields with repetitive/sequential data, such as repeated text, dates, and numbers.

Autofill Dates

To autofill a set of dates in a specific order:

Steps:

- In a cell, write the initial Date of the series.

- Drag the handle in the cell's bottom-right corner down quite so many cells as you'd want to fill.

Autofill Numbers

To autofill a set of integers in a specific order:

Steps:

- In a cell, write the first number in the series.

- In the adjacent cell, enter the second number in the series.

- By moving the mouse over both cells, you may select them.

- Click and drag the handle in the bottom-right corner of the second cell to fill as many cells as you wish.

To automatically fill a column/row of cells with the same number or text:

- In a cell, type the number or text.

- Drag the handle in the cell's bottom-right corner over that many cells as you'd want to fill.

Alternating Numbers & Text with Autofill

To fill many cells at once, utilize the autofill function. Type the seven days of the week into 7 adjacent cells in a column/row, for example, to produce a repeating list of days of the week. Select

the seven cells you wish to fill, then click the handle in the bottom-right corner of the last cell and drag it across as many cells as you like.

Autofill Functions1

Functions can be copied using Autofill. Columns A and B in the example below contain lists of numbers, but column C has the sum of columns A & B for each row. "=SUM(A2:B2)" would be the function in cell C2. Follow these steps to duplicate this function to other cells in column C:

Steps:

- Choose the cell in which the function you wish to duplicate is located. In this case,

- Drag the handle in the cell's bottom-right corner down as many cells as you'd want to fill. For each of the rows selected in the example below, the total of columns A & B can now be found in column C.

2.9 Charts

Using a number of graph types, charts allow you to show data input into a worksheet in the visual style. You must first enter the data in a worksheet before creating a chart.

The Chart Wizard

To create a chart:

Steps:

- Fill out a worksheet with your information.

- Select the cells, including the headers, that you wish to include in the chart.

- Select Insert from the drop-down menu. Excel offers a variety of chart types in the Charts category, including column, line, bar, pie, area, scatter, and other charts.

- When you choose the chart type you desire, a menu will appear with more chart styles available within that category.

- Choose a chart style from the drop-down menu. The graph will appear in your spreadsheet.

Resizing a Chart

To resize your chart:

Steps:

- To pick a chart, click on it. Around the chart box, an eight-handle border will emerge.

- Drag chart to its new size by clicking one of the handles.

Moving a Chart

To move the chart:

Steps:

- To pick a chart, click on it.

- Move your mouse over the chart box's edge until the cursor turns to a ⊕.

- Drag the chart towards its new spot by clicking and dragging it.

Moving Chart Elements

You may also change the order of the chart's parts, such as the title, labels, & visuals. To move components within a chart, do the following:

- To move an element, simply click it. It will be surrounded by a boundary.

- Continue to move the mouse across the boundary until the cursor turns to a ⊕

- Transfer the element to its new home.

Formatting a Chart

The Chart Tools bar would display across the ribbon once you've built a chart or selected your chart. The Layout, Design,

& Format tabs on the Chart Tools bar are handy for editing and customizing your chart. The Layout tab allows you to adjust a chart's axes and gridlines, align the labels and legend, and arrange the chart's backdrop. You may modify the style of the chart using the Design tab. You may modify the style of chart elements, such as the shape & text styles, using the Format tab. A small list of more particular features that may be accessible via the Design, Layout, and Format tabs is provided below.

To format an item on the chart, click the object on chart or choose the object from the Format tab's Chart Elements dropdown menu. A window with the object's properties will open, allowing you to make formatting adjustments.

Change Chart Type, On the Design tab, click Change Chart Type button to change the chart type. The Chart Legend button, found on the Layout tab, lets you choose where the legend appears on your chart and whether it is visible. Display Data by Column or Row, On the Design tab, click the Switch Row/Column button to display the data by column or row.

Copying a Chart to Microsoft Word

Follow these procedures to copy a completed chart into a Microsoft Word document:

Steps:

- By clicking on the chart, you may choose it.

- To copy something, click Copy.

- Open the MS Word document into which you'd like to paste the graph.

- Press the Paste button.

2.10 Quick Access Toolbar

You may create a toolbar in Excel that contains the functions you use the most. The Quick Access Toolbar helps you to do your most popular tasks swiftly and conveniently.

Steps:

- Click the File tab in the upper left corner of your screen.

- Select Options.

- Click Customize in the left sidebar. The customization choices for your Quick Access Toolbar should appear.

To add a command to your toolbar:

Steps:

- Choose a command from the left-hand scrolling menu.

- Select Add from the drop-down menu. The command has now been added to the right-hand list. The up & down arrows on the right of the window can be used to reorganize the commands on the toolbar.

- Select Show Quick Access Toolbar from the drop-down menu underneath the Ribbon box.

- Click the OK button. Below the Ribbon, your Quick Access Toolbar now will show.

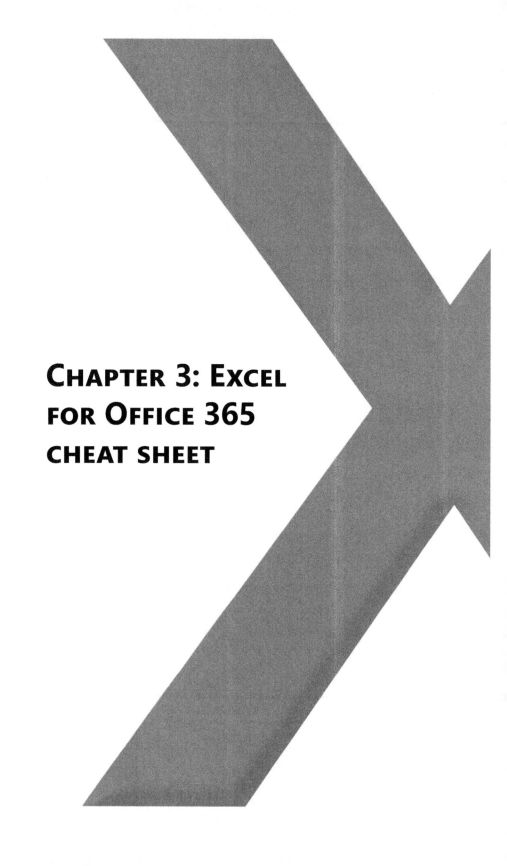

CHAPTER 3: EXCEL FOR OFFICE 365 CHEAT SHEET

Although Microsoft Windows receives a lot of headlines, when it comes to getting actual work done, you focus on the apps that run on it. And if you work with spreadsheets, you're probably using Excel.

Excel is, of course, a component of Microsoft's Office productivity package. Individuals & businesses can either pay for the software license upfront & own it forever (what Microsoft refers to as the "perpetual" version of suite), or they can buy an Office 365 membership, which gives them access to software for as long as they keep paying subscription fee.

When you buy a perpetual edition of the suite, such as Office 2019 or Office 2016, the programs will never be updated with new features, but Office 365 apps will be updated on a regular basis.

This cheat sheet will keep you up to date on the new capabilities in Office 365's MS Excel for "Windows" pc clients that have been released since 2015.

3.1 Use the Ribbon

The Ribbon interface, which you may have grown to love (or despise) in previous versions of Excel, is still functional. Since Office 2007, Ribbon has been integrated into Office programs.

Microsoft changed the design of the Ribbon in September 2018. It's now flatter, with high-contrast color that makes the Ribbon's symbols and text easier to view. The top green bar has been removed, and the tab names are now shown on a grey backdrop.

Recommended whitepapers

- The Demands of a Hyper-Connected Enterprise are met by a Next-Generation Network. IVAULT

Excel for Office 365 now features a cleaner Ribbon with easier-to-read icons and text.

A Help option has been added to the right of the View tab, which is a small alteration to the Ribbon layout. Download the Excel for Office 365 Ribbon quick reference to learn which commands are located on which tabs on the Ribbon. It's also worth noting that you can discover commands using the Ribbon's search box.

Press Ctrl-F1 to remove the Ribbon instructions, just as you would in previous versions of Excel. (The tabs above the Ribbon, such as File, Home, Insert, and so on, remain visible.) Ctrl-F1 will bring them back to life.

There are various ways to display Ribbon as well. To access them, go to the top right of the screen & select Ribbon Display Options button, which is just to the left of the icons for shrinking and maximizing PowerPoint. These three selections appear in a drop-down menu:

- Auto-hide Ribbon: Hides the whole Ribbon, as well as the tabs & commands beneath it. Click at top of Excel to bring up the Ribbon again.

- Show Tabs: This reveals the tabs while hiding the instructions beneath them. It's the same as hitting Ctrl-F1 on your keyboard. When commands beneath the tabs are hidden, push Ctrl-F1, tap the tab, or select "Show Tabs and Commands" from the Ribbon display button.

- Show Commands and Tabs: This option displays both the tabs & the commands.

You may also change the title bar's color to black, white, or dark grey if the lovely green hue is too much for you. To get started, go to File > Options and then General from the drop-down

menu. Click the down arrow next to Office Theme in the "Personalize your copy of Microsoft Office" section, and choose Dark Gray, white, or black from the drop-down menu. Instead, select "Colorful" from the drop-down list to make the title bar green again. A drop-down selection for Office Background is located just above Office Theme menu. In the title bar, you may select to display a design like a circuit board/circles & stripe.

When you select the File tab on Ribbon, you'll see a valuable feature called the backstage area, which displays when you click the File tab. You can view the cloud-based customer services you have connected to the Office account, including such SharePoint & OneDrive, if you choose Open or Save a Copy from the menu on the left. Each location now has its own email address shown beneath it. This is particularly useful if you utilize a cloud service with several accounts, such as if you have a personal OneDrive account and a corporate OneDrive account. You'll be able to tell which is which at a look.

3.2 Search to get tasks done quickly

Excel is not even the most user-friendly among software with so many sophisticated capabilities, and it may be difficult to make sense of them all. According to Microsoft tell You, a new expanded search function in Excel 2016 makes finding even the most hidden tool in the spreadsheet simpler. However, the functionality has been renamed Searching by Microsoft, and it continues to function in the same manner.

Use it by typing a search term into the Search box that appears to the right of all tab headings on the Ribbon. The letter Q may be substituted for Q on a keyboard. You may then enter an action to perform, such as "build a pivot table," into the search box. When you click on the job, you'll be presented with possible matches. You'll notice that the first outcome is a real correlation to the form of making a Level of granularity click on it, and you'll be sent directly to the PivotTable creation form rather than needing to go to the Insert tab on your Toolbar first.

The search box makes it easy to perform just about any task in Excel. (Click the image to enlarge.) If you'd like more information about your task, the last two items in the menu allow you to choose from related Support topics or explore for your word working with Smart Lookup. (Further on Smart Lookup beneath.)

Even if you think yourself as a worksheet jockey, it will be worth your time seeking out the improved search function. It is a huge time-saver & far more effective than looking through a Ribbon to locate a command.

Also helpful is that it recalls the features you have previously snapped on in the box, so you first find a list of earlier tasks you have searched for when you click on it. That be sure that tasks you frequently accomplish are always within simple reach. In addition, it makes jobs that you only seldom perform accessible and convenient.

As previously stated, the query bar is not restricted to looking for tasks. Bing may also be used to include searches, and customers with Microsoft office 365 accounts can apply it to seek corporate connections and documents saved in OneDrive or SharePoint.

3.3 Smart Lookup

When you're doing internet research, Smart Lookup can help you. The Smart Lookup tool, for example, allows you to do inquiries as you're creating a worksheet. Choose Smart Lookup first from the selection that displays when you right-click a column that contains a keyword or set of words.

While you're doing it, Excel enables Microsoft's Bing search tool to conduct internet research on the phrase or terms in concern and then presents definitions, any relevant Wikipedia articles, and some other findings from the web in the Smart Lookup window, which shows on the right of the image. View the single spread of any search result by clicking on a link. The Explain tab on the pane will provide you with a simple meaning of the term. Click on the Search tab in the main window to gather more information.

"Payback period" and "return on investment" are good examples of general words that may be used. Expect Smart Lookup to not always perform well when investigating financial facts that you would include in the spreadsheets.

For instance, if You searched for "Consumer price index in French 2018," the very first result returned was the Wikipedia article for France, but it was not until the third article that you were able to get precise information regarding France's consumer price index for 2018. While searching for "Steel output United States," Smart Lookup provided me with the results I was looking for in seconds. As a result, even if it doesn't always strike the mark when finding financial data, it's useful to start with it. Also, consider that Microsoft is always improving its artificial intelligence capacities in Office, which means that

Smart Lookup has become more accurate with age. It's important to note that, to fully utilize Smart Lookup in Xls or any other Office application, you may first need to activate Microsoft's clever services function, which gathers your keyword phrases and certain information from your worksheets and other Office documents. If you're worried about your privacy, you ought to decide if the privacy risk is acceptable for the simplicity of doing an inquiry from inside the app. Using Smart Lookup will prompt you to activate it if you haven't already done so. Afterward, it will be enabled across all of your Microsoft Programs.

3.4 Keyboard shortcuts are quite convenient.

There's excellent news for those who like keyboard shortcut buttons: Excel has a plethora of them. The most helpful ones are highlighted in the table beneath, and there are many more to be found on the Microsoft Office website. Useful Excel keyboard shortcuts:

KEY COMBINATION	ACTION
Worksheet navigation	
PgUp / PgDn	Move the cursor on the screen up or down.
Alt-PgUp / Alt-PgDn	Move the cursor on the screen to the left/right
Ctrl-PgUp / Ctrl-PgDn	Change the orientation of one worksheet tab to the left or right.
Up / Down arrow key	One cell can be moved up or down.
Tab	Make your way to the next cell on the right.
Shift-Tab	Move to the cell on the left-hand side of the grid.
Home	Return to the start of a new row of characters
Ctrl-Home	Change the position of the cursor to the start of a worksheet
Ctrl-End	Next, go on to the final cell that contains information.
Ctrl-Left arrow	When in a cell, drag the cursor to the word on the left.
Ctrl-Right arrow	Move your cursor to the word to the right when within a cell.
Ctrl-G or F5	The Go-To dialogue box will be shown.

KEY COMBINATION	ACTION
F6	It is possible to switch among worksheets, Ribbons, task panes, and Zoom controls.
Ctrl-F6	If you have more than a single worksheet active, click on the next to continue.

Ribbon navigation

Alt	Ribbon shortcuts are shown.
Alt-F	Navigate to the File tab
Alt-H	Navigate to the Home tab.
Alt-N	Navigate to the Insert tab
Alt-P	Navigate to the Page Layout tab
Alt-M	Navigate to the Formulas tab
Alt-A	Navigate to the Data tab
Alt-R	Navigate to the Review tab
Alt-W	Navigate to the View tab
Alt-Q	Insert the cursor into the Search box.
Alt-JC	Once the cursor is over a chart, click on the Chart Design tab.
Alt-JA	Navigate to the Format tab when the cursor is on a chart
Alt-JT	Navigate to the Table Design tab when the cursor is on a table

KEY COMBINATION	ACTION
Alt-JP	Navigate to the Picture Format tab when the cursor is on an image
Alt-JI	Navigate to the Draw tab
Alt-B	Navigate to the Power Pivot tab

Working with Data

Shift-Spacebar	Choose a row
Ctrl-Spacebar	Choose a column
Ctrl-A or Ctrl-Shift-Spacebar	Choose an entire worksheet
Shift-Arrow key	Increase selection by a single cell
Shift-PgDn / Shift-PgUp	Expand selection down one screen / up one screen
Shift-Home	Stretch selection to the beginning of a row
Ctrl-Shift-Home	Lengthen selection to the beginning of the worksheet
Ctrl-C	Copy cell's matters to the clipboard
Ctrl-X	Copy and delete cell subjects
Ctrl-V	Paste from the clipboard into a cell
Ctrl-Alt-V	Show the Paste Special dialog box

KEY COMBINATION	ACTION
Enter	Complete the data entry in a cell and go on to the next cell along the row.
Shift-Enter	Complete the data entry in a cell and go on to the next cell along the row.
Esc	Terminate your entry into a cell
Ctrl-;	Insert the present date
Ctrl-Shift-;	Insert the present time
Ctrl-T or Ctrl-L	Show the Create Table dialog box
Ctrl-End	When you're in the formula bar, drag the mouse pointer to the end of the paragraph you're editing.
Ctrl-Shift-End	Pick all words from the pointer to the end of the line in the formula bar.
Alt-F8	Edit, run, Create, or delete a macro

Formatting cells and data

Ctrl-1	Show the Format Cells dialog box
Alt-'	Show the Style dialog box
Ctrl-Shift-&	Use a border to a cell or selection

KEY COMBINATION	ACTION
Ctrl-Shift-_	Eliminate a border from a cell or selection
Ctrl-Shift-$	Use the Currency format with two decimal places
Ctrl-Shift-~	Use the Number format
Ctrl-Shift-%	Use the % format with no decimal places
Ctrl-Shift-#	Use the Date format using day, month, and year
Ctrl-Shift-@	Use the Time format using the 12-hour clock
Ctrl-K	Add a hyperlink
Ctrl-Q	Showing Quick Analysis choices for cells that include information that has been chosen.

Working with formulas

=	Start a formula
Alt-=	AutoSum should be included.
Shift-F3	Functions should be added.
Ctrl-`	The display of formulae and cell values may be toggled on and off.
Ctrl-'	Make a copy / paste the equation from above into the serving cell.

KEY COMBINATION	ACTION
F9	Calculate the sum of all work-sheets in all active workbooks
Shift-F9	Evaluate the existing worksheet
Ctrl-Shift-U	Increase or collapse the formula bar

Other useful shortcuts

Ctrl-N	Build a new workbook
Ctrl-O	Start a workbook
Ctrl-S	Save a workbook
Ctrl-W	Shut down a workbook
Ctrl-P	Print a workbook
Ctrl-F	Show the Replace and Find dialog box
Ctrl-Z	Negate the last action
Ctrl-Y	Redo the last action
Shift-F2	Insertion or edit a cell comment
Ctrl-Shift-O	Choose all cells which contain comments
Ctrl-9	Hide selected rows
Ctrl-Shift-	Unhide secret rows in a choice
Ctrl-0	Hide chosen columns

KEY COMBINATION	**ACTION**
Ctrl-Shift-)	Unhide any concealed columns in a choice that have been hidden.
F7	Check the spelling of the current worksheet or the specified range.

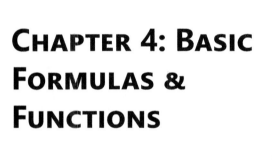

CHAPTER 4: BASIC FORMULAS & FUNCTIONS

4.1 What is Excel Formula?

An equation in Microsoft Excel is a statement that works on the data contained inside a range of cells. This formula always returns a result, even if the consequence is an error. You can conduct equations such as adding, subtraction, multiplying, and dividing with the help of Excel formulae and functions. In addition to these functions, you can use Excel to compute averages and % for a range of cells, modify the date and time variables, and perform various other tasks.

There's also another phrase that Excel formulae are quite acquainted with, the terminology "function. " Formulas & functions are two things that are occasionally used similarly. They are strongly linked, yet they are also distinct. The equal symbol (=) marks the beginning of a formula. Meantime, functions are often used to conduct complicated computations that are impossible to complete by hand. The names of Excel functions are intended to convey the purpose for which they are being used.

The following example demonstrates how to manually multiply two numbers using the '*' operator and the multiplication formula.

| C2 | | | | | f_x | =A2*B2 |

	A	B	C
1	Qty	Price per Unit	Total Sales (Using Formula)
2	10	30	300
3	11	35	385
4	12	40	480

The following example demonstrates how we may execute a multiplier with the help of the function 'PRODUCT..' As you've seen, we won't make use of the arithmetic operator in this situation.

Excel formulas & functions enable you to do your activities more efficiently and effectively, saving you time. As we go, we'll learn about the many sorts of functions accessible in Excel and how to employ suitable formulae when the situation calls for them.

4.2 Formulas & functions in Microsoft Excel

The type of function you wish to conduct on the dataset will determine which Excel formulas & functions you need to use in your spreadsheet. It is planned to include arithmetic operations, identity functions, data & time, sum function, and a few lookup functions, among other topics.

Consider the following list of the top 25 Excel formulae that you must know. In this post, we've subdivided 25 Excel formulae into groups depending on the actions they perform. Let's begin with the first Excel formula on the collection, number one.

1. SUM

The SUM() function, like the title suggests, returns the sum of the values ranging in cells that have been chosen. It is responsible for performing the mathematical approach of addition. Here's an illustration of what It means :

	A	B	C	D
			f_x	=SUM(C2:C4)
1	Qty	Price per Unit	Total Sales	
2	10	30	300	
3	11	35	385	
4	12	40	480	
5		Total	1165	

As you can see in the example above, all we had to do to get the overall number of sales for each unit was enter in the function "=SUM(C2:C4)." It automatically generates the numbers 300, 385, and 480 together. C5 contains the outcome of the calculation.

2. THE AVERAGE

The AVERAGE() function is concerned with computing the median of a series of cell values that have been specified. To discover the average of all sales, write "AVERAGE(C2, C3, C4)" into the search box, as shown in the example below. It quickly takes the average for you, and you may save the result in any place you like.

3. COUNT

The COUNT() function calculates the cell density in a range of cell types with a numeric value. It does not include empty cells or the cells that hold information in any other style than the form of the number.

We measure from C1 to C4, which is an optimal number of cells. However, since its COUNT function only directly impacts cells having numeric data, the result is 3 because the cell holding "Total Sales" has been removed from this calculation. If you need to count all of the cells that contain numeric data, words, or any other kind of file format, you must employ the 'COUNTA()' method in your spreadsheet. COUNTA(), on the other hand, doesn't quite count any null cells. COUNTBLANK() is a function that measures the number of empty cells present in a given range of cells.

4. SUBTITLE TOTAL

Moving on, let's now learn how the summary function works. The SUBTOTAL() method returns the subtotal of a collection of records in a database. Depending on your needs, you may choose from various options, including average, count, total, min, max, min, and others. Examine the following two illustrations. In the above sample, we did the subtotal analysis on cells spanning A2 to A4, and the result was A2. As you've seen, the function that was applied is "=SUBTOTAL(1, A2: A4)," where "1" refers to the aggregate in the subtotal list. Because of this, the function mentioned above will return the average of A2:A4, and the response to it will be 11, which will be put in C5.

Similar to this, "=SUBTOTAL(4, A2: A4)" picks the cell with the greatest sum of the values in cells A2 through A4, which is 12. Putting the number "4" into the function yields the best possible outcome.

C5				f_x	=SUBTOTAL(4,A2:A4)	
	A	B	C		D	E
1	Qty	Price per Unit	Total Sales			
2	10	30	300			
3	11	35	385			
4	12	40	480			
5		Subtotal	12			

Figure 5: The Count function in Microsoft Excel.

5. MODULUS

The MOD() function is responsible for returning the residual when a divisor of some kind splits a given integer. To further comprehend the concepts, let's peek at the examples provided below. We have calculated the number 10 by the number three during the first instance. The remaining is determined using the equation "=MOD(A2,3)". The result is saved in the B2 variable. Alternatively, we may write "=MOD(10,3)" to get the same result as typing the whole expression.

In opposition, we have split 12 by 4 in this case. The balance is equal to zero, and it is placed in B3.

6. POWER

If an integer is raised to the appropriate power, the output is returned by the method "Power()." Take a look at the following samples to see what It means: So you can see from the example above that to discover the strength of 10 contained in A2 increased to 3, we must enter "= POWER (A2,3)." It is how the Excel power function is implemented.

7. CEILING

Then there's the function that raises the ceiling. The CEILING() function increases the importance of an integer by rounding it up to the closest multiple of significance. For the number 35.316, the next largest multiple of 5 is 40.

8. FLOOR

In contrast to the ceiling service, the minimal floor difference is

a number to the smallest multiple of importance it may be represented by.

9. CONCATENATE

The smallest multiple of 5 that can be found for 35.316 is 35.9. CONCATENATE. This method combines or unites some text strings to form a single text string. The many approaches to carrying out this duty are detailed below.

In this sample, we used the syntax =CONCATENATE to accomplish our goal. We have used the syntax =CONCATENATE throughout this instance to accomplish our goal (A27&" "&B27).

Those were the two approaches to implementing the combination operation in Excel discussed.

10. LEN

The LEN() function returns the total set of entries contained inside a string. As a result, it will count all symbols, including spaces & special characters, in the input.

11. REPLACE WITH A NEW ONE

It is named because it works on replacing a portion of an existing text string with another portion of an existing text string. '=REPLACE(old text, start num, num chars, new text)' is the formula to be used. This difference leads to the index point where you wish to begin changing the letters with new ones. Following that, num chars specify the number of words you wish to replace with another.

Look at some of the several ways we may use this function. Using the code "=REPLACE(A15,1,1, "B"), we are replacing the letter A101 with the letter B101. After that, we'll change A102 with A2102 by entering "=REPLACE(A16,1,1, "A2")" on the command line.

We will quickly replace Adam with Saam by inserting "=REPLACE(A17,1,2, "Sa")" in the code. Fig. Excel's Replace function in action.

12. SUBSTITUTE

Text strings are replaced with fresh text using the SUBSTITUTE() method, which is defined as follows:

"=SUBSTITUTE(text, old text, new text, [instance num])" is the syntax for this function. Multiple times in this book, the term [instance num] relates to the index number of the current texts.

A few instances of this function are shown below. "I like" has been replaced with the phrase "He likes" by entering "=SUBSTI-TUTE(A20, "I like," "He likes")" in this case.

B21	f_x =SUBSTITUTE(A21,2010, 2016,2)	
	A	B
19	Substitute	
20	I like Excel	He likes Excel
21	MS Excel 2010, MS Word 2010	MS Excel 2010, MS Word 2016
22	MS Excel 2010, MS Word 2010	MS Excel 2016, MS Word 2016

Figure: Excel's substitute feature.

By entering "=SUBSTITUTE(A21,2010,2016,2)," we are replacing the 2nd 2010 in the original document in cell A21 with the year 2016, as seen in the following example. Then, by putting "=SUB-STITUTE(A22,2010,2016)," we are substituting the 2010s in the original document with the current year.

Figure 1: Excel's substitute feature. Now that we've covered the replace function, let's move along to the next function on the checklist.

13. THE LEFT, RIGHT, AND MIDDLE

The LEFT() method returns the set of entries that have been re-moved from the beginning of a text string. The MID() method, on the other hand, returns the letters from the center of a string of text, given the beginning point and length of the text string. Ul-timately, the right() method returns the set of entries remaining before the conclusion of a text string is reached. Let's look at a few examples to better comprehend these functions. In the fol-lowing example, we will use the function left to acquire the left-most term on the paragraph in cell A5 by using the function left.

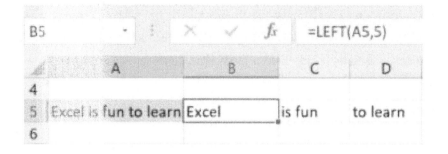

Figure: Excel's left-hand function

The following is an example of how to use the mid function.

	A	B	C	D
4				
5	Excel is fun to learn	Excel	is fun	to learn
6				

CS f_x =MID(A5,7,6)

Figure: Excel's Mid function in action

Here's an example of how to do the correct function.

	A	B	C	D
4				
5	Excel is fun to learn	Excel	is fun	to learn
6				

D5 f_x =RIGHT(A5,8)

Figure: Excel's right-hand function.

14. UPPER, LOWER, AND CORRECT

Using the UPPER () method, it is possible to transform any text string into uppercase using the UPPER() method. The LOWER() method, on the other hand, is used to transform any text string to small. In the case of text strings, the PROPER() method changes them to proper case, which means that just the first word of each sentence will be in the capital, and all the remaining letters will be in lowercase. Let's look at some instances to help us better comprehend what it is saying: It is an example of converting a lowercase text in A6 to a complete uppercase text in A7.

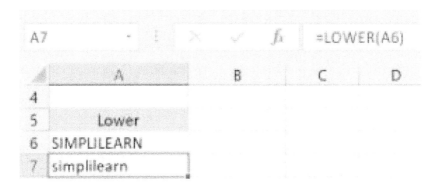

As shown in A7, we have transformed the words in A6 into a complete lowercase font.

In Excel, the lower function is shown in Figure. The inappropriate text in A6 has been transformed into a clean & appropriate format in A7, and we have completed the project.

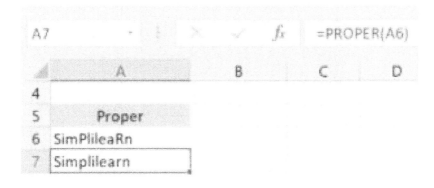

Figure: Excel's appropriate function

Now, let's look at some of the date and time operations available in Excel.

15. RIGHT NOW ()

The NOW() function in Excel displays the time and date on the computer system. Fig: The feature in Excel is now available.

The outcome of the NOW() function will vary depending on the current time and date on your machine.

16. TODAY ()

The TODAY () function in Excel displays the date and time currently displayed on the system. Figure: Today's function in Microsoft Excel To determine the day of the month, the method DAY() is required. It would be a number between 1 and 31 in the range. The month's start day is January 1, and the end day of the month is December 31.

The year is returned by the YEAR() function, which, as its name implies, produces the year from a current value. The YEAR() function, as the name suggests, returns the year from a date value.

Figure: The Year function in Microsoft Excel

17. TIME()

This method transforms hours, minutes, and seconds that are supplied as integers to an Excel product code written in a system time using the TIME() function.

Figure: Excel's time function

18. HOUR, MINUTE, SECOND

The HOUR() function calculates an hour from such a present value expressed as a number between 0 and 23. 0 denotes midnight, whereas 23 denotes 11 p.m. The method MINUTE() generates the minute like a range between 0 and 59 from a present value. The SECOND() function compares the second like an integer between 0 and 59 from a present value. Figure: Excel's second function

19. DATEDIF

The DATEDIF() function calculates the alteration in years, months, or days between two dates. It calculates a person's current age founded on two dates: their birth date and today's date.

20. VLOOKUP

The VLOOKUP() function comes next in this section. It stands for the vertical lookup responsible for looking for a particular value in the leftmost column of a table. The value of a column you specify is then returned in the same row.

The VLOOKUP stored procedure assertions are as follows:

- Lookup value - This is the value you need to look for in the table's first column.

- This parameter indicates the table from which the value is retrieved.

- Col index - The column from which the value should be retrieved in the table.

- [Optional] range lookup TRUE indicates a close match. EXACT MATCH = FALSE.

There will be a use of the table below to understand how the VLOOKUP function works. You could use the VLOOKUP function to determine Stuart's department, as shown below:

VLOOKUP is an Excel function that allows you to look up information. The lookup value is in cell A11, the table array is in cell A2, the column index number with department information is in cell 3, and the range lookup is in cell 0.

If you press enter, "Advertising" will appear, indicating that Scott is a member of the marketing department.

9			Vlookup		
10	First Name	Last Name	Department	City	Date Hired
11	Stuart		Marketing		

21. HLOOKUP

HLOOKUP(), or horizontal lookup, is a function similar to VLOOKUP(). HLOOKUP searches the top row of a table or myriad benefits for a value. It returns the value from a specified row in the same column.

The HLOOKUP function's parameters are as follows:

- lookup value - This is the Data that will be looked up.

- Table - The database from which you must obtain information.

- Row index - The row integer from which data should be retrieved.

- [optional] range lookup This binary value indicates whether the match is precise or approximate. The return value is TRUE, which indicates a close match.

- Let's examine how to use HLOOKUP to discover the town of Jenson in the table below.

- M5 represents the database array, 4 denotes the rows identification number, and 0 denotes a close match.

- It will reply "New York" after you press enter.

22. IF

If a condition is TRUE, the IF() function tests it and returns a specific value. If the criteria are FALSE, it will return a different result.

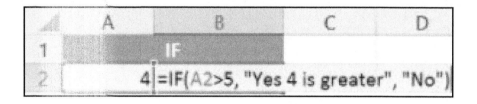

We need to see whether the number in cell A2 is bigger than 5 in the instance below. If the value is larger than 5, the method will return "Yes 4 is greater," otherwise "No."

Figure: Excel's If function

Because 4 is not larger than 5, it will respond 'No' in this scenario. Another often used function is 'IFERROR.' If a decision making to a failure, this method returns a value; otherwise, it delivers the expression's value.

Assume you wish to divide ten by zero. It is incorrect because you can't split an integer by zero. There will be an error as a consequence. "Cannot divide" will be returned by the following method.

23. INDEX-MATCH

The INDEX-MATCH method returns a value from the leftmost column. You can't go back to an assessment from a right-hand column using VLOOKUP. One advantage of index-match over

VLOOKUP is that VLOOKUP requires more computing power from Excel. It is since it must assess the complete table array you've picked. Excel needs to examine the search and output columns when using INDEX-MATCH. Let's look at how to determine the city where Jenson lives using the data below.

Fig: Index-Match function in Excel Now, let's treasure the subdivision of Zampa.

24. COUNTIF

COUNTIF() is a function that counts the cell count in a region that satisfies a criterion. A coronavirus sampling database including Data on coronavirus incidence and fatalities in each nation and area can be found below. Let's see how many times Afghanistan appears in the table.

Figure: Excel's Countif method

The COUNTIFS method counts the total number of cells specified by a collection of circumstances. If you wish to keep track of how many days, more than 100 instances in India have been there, the COUNTIFS method may be used in the following way.

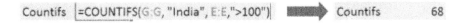

25. SUMIF

SUMIF() sums the cells indicated by a qualifier or criterion. The coronavirus information below will calculate the overall number of instances in India until June 3, 2020. (We have data from December 31, 2020, to June 3, 2020, in our database.)

| Sumif | =SUMIF(G:G, "India",E:E) | ➡ | Sumif | 2076158 |

Excel›s Sumif function

The SUMIFS() among these are the cells that a set of circumstances or requirements specifies. Let's look at the overall number of instances in France on days less than 100 dead.

| Sumifs | =SUMIFS(E:E,G:G,"France",F:F,"<100") | ➡ | Sumifs | 20638 |

CHAPTER 5:
ADVANCED
FORMULAS &
FUNCTIONS

Goal Seek is a method in Fundamental Excel Functions that enables you to change the parameters to acquire the expected result. To achieve a future conclusion, the technique relies on the trial-and-error approach.

Let's have a basic example to help you understand.

Example

In this case, we would like to know the cost of borrowing if the client wishes to spend $5000 each month to pay back the mortgage. You'll utilize the PMT method whenever you want to figure out how much money you'll need to pay every month to pay off your debt.

Let's walk through this issue stepwise to see how you can figure out the rate of interest that would pay off a $400,000 loan with a $5,000 monthly payment. The PMT equation should be put next to the Pay cell. Since there is currently no number inside the interest rates box, Excel calculates a payment of $3,333.33 based on the assumption that the cost of borrowing is 0%. Do not pay attention to it.

- Go to Data > Anything - If Analysis > Goal Seek

		f_x	=PMT(D7/12,D6,D5)		
B	C	D	E	F
	Loan Amount	$400,000.00		
	Terms In Month	120		
	Rate of Interest			
	Payment	($3,333.33)		

- Set the monthly premium to a negative amount of $5,000. The low value is represented as a reduction in the amount.

- Set the moving cell to the interest rate.

- Click the OK button. You'll see that the target seek device calculates the interest rate necessary to repay the loan.

- Change the setting to % under Home > Number.

Your conclusion will look like the below:

Loan Amount	$400,000.00
Terms In Month	120
Rate of Interest	9%
Payment	($5,000.00)

Solver's What-If Analysis

What-If Analysis is a way of modifying variables in Equipment formulae to test out alternative situations. Several distinct sets of values may be utilized in one or more of these Advanced Excel formulae to investigate various outcomes.

For what analysis, a solution was ideal. It's a Microsoft Excel insert that's useful on various levels. The characteristic may be used to find the best possible result for an equation in the goal cell. However, other equation cell entries in a worksheet are subject to some limitations or limits.

The solver uses decision variables, a collection of cells that are utilized to compute the formulae in the goal and restriction cells. To operate on the constraints on restriction cells, the solver alters the number of discrete state cells. This procedure assists in defining the goal cell's intended outcome.

- Using the Solver Add-in

- Select Options from the File tab.

- Choose Solver Add-in from the Add-ins menu and click the Go option.

- Crisscross Solver Add-in and click OK.

- In the Data tag, you can see the Solver alternative is added in the Evaluate group.

5.2 How to Use Solver in Excel

We'll look for a solution to simple optimal solution in this instance.

Problem: Assume you're a business owner who wants to earn $8000 per year.

Objective: Determine the number of units to sell and the unit price to complete the tasks.

For instance, we developed the following model:

- Press the Solver button within the Evaluation group on the Insert tab.

- Choose the income cell within the specific goal and change its significance to $8000.

- Choose the C5, C6, and C10 cells to alter the varying cell.

- Click the Solve button.

- Depending on the circumstances, your database schema will change.

5.3 If-Else

The IF method is often used to check the circumstance and generate results if this is true and a different number if false.

Syntax = IF is the syntax (test, true result, false result)

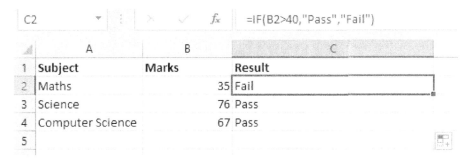

5.4 If-Error

If a calculation causes a problem, the Xls IFERROR process gives an alternate result. When no error is identified, it delivers the intended result.

Syntax = IFERROR (value, value if error)

When an equation attempts to distribute an amount by zero, Excel returns a split by zero.

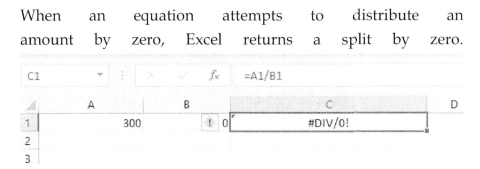

If the equation analyses to an error, you can use the IFERROR purpose to add a text.

5.5 Tables with pivots

A pivot table is an Excel format concise overview tool that allows you to document and discover trend lines based on your statistics accurately in a short period. You may create a section-by-section summary using the pivot table's drag and drop functionality and the appropriate functions therein. Data from a Sample. We'll utilize the example data, consisting of 41 entries with five areas of consumer data. This information is ideal for comprehending the pivot table.

5.6 Insert Pivot Tables

Follow the instructions underneath to add a pivot table to your spreadsheet:

- Every cell in a data collection may be selected by clicking on it.

- Choose PivotTable in the Tables category on the Design tab.

- There will be a dialogue box that appears. Your information will be auto-selected by Excel. In addition, a new spreadsheet for the pivot table will be created.

- Click the OK button. Then it will generate a pivot grid worksheet.

5.7 Drag and Drop Fields

Drag the fields below to the regions to obtain the total number of products purchased by each customer.

- From the Buyer field to the Rows area.

- From the Items field to the Values box.

5.8 VBA in Excel

VBA is the abbreviation for Visual Basic Analysis. Microsoft's incident software program for Office programmed is Excel VBA. Most individuals who create VBA code employ macros. Excel's Development Option should be enabled. The Development firm tab is kept secret by mistake on the Ribbon, and also to customize the Ribbon, follow the steps below: Right-click wherever on the Ribbon, then select Personalize the Ribbon from the menu.

Go to Modify the Ribbon and pick the Developer checkbox.

The interface of the VBA Editor

You can access the VBA interaction by pressing ALT + F11 on your keypad or by going to the Design tab or selecting Visual Basic. Creating a Start Button and associating it with a Macro.

Let's start by using the command button to create a macro within a week of empowering the developer tab and acquainting ourselves with the VBA editor. You must follow the steps outlined below to add a command button to the spreadsheet you are starting to work with:

- Select Developer > Insert > ActiveX Controls > Command from the drop-down menu.

- On your worksheet, drag the command button.

- Here's what to do to add a macro to the user clicking:

- Choose View Code from the context menu when you right-click on the instruction buttons.

- Add the ensuing lines of code shown below.

- Exit the VBA editor and go to the worksheet's user clicking. Assure the design mode is turned off.

5.9 Matching and Indexing

It is an Excel Advance function. The MATCH method returns the location of a value inside a given range, whereas the INDEX condition returns a particular value within a one-dimensional range. The MATCH method returns the ID you're seeking for's location. The INDEX function will return the pay figure for the job.

Function of Offset

The OFFSET method returns a connection to several cellular cells combined with information of rows or columns away.

Syntax: OFFSET

Example:

- Take the following information into consideration:

- Starting at A1, refer to C4 as follows: A1 rows 3, and cols 2:

5.10 SUM Function With OFFSET

We got 2 years of monthly sales reports in this instance. The purpose is to calculate the total revenue for a given month. The OFFSET method provides a 1x2 region with 8 rows beneath cell A2 and 1 line right of it. The total of this region is then calculated using the SUM function.

CHAPTER 6:
PIVOT TABLES
IN EXCEL

6.1 What is a Pivot Table, and how does it work?

Among the most basic data analysis techniques is the pivot table. Numerous essential business queries can be quickly answered using pivot tables. We construct Pivot Tables for many purposes, one of which is to send data. We want to back up our narrative with simple information to comprehend and see. Even though Pivot Tables are just tables with no true visuals, people can still be used to tell a story visually.

Do you want to start with pivot tables?

Experiment with pivot tables first to gain a deeper understanding of what we're talking about. After that, you're free to continue reading. More examples can be found by proceeding to the book.

What is the best way to learn how to use pivot tables?

Mastering pivot tables may appear to be a difficult task. You could comprehend it very well if you comprehend a few basic principles. You could indeed quickly catch up with your more knowledgeable coworkers in this area. But also, of curriculum, you'll be able to command a better income on the employment market. What is a Pivot Table, and how does it work? The

The'remainder of this guide will walk you through it step by step, utilizing principles you're already acquainted with...

6.2 What is the purpose of pivot?

What are the benefits of using a pivot table?

A Pivot Table is a tool for analyzing, sorting, restructuring, grouping, counting, totaling, or averaging data in a table. It permits us to change rows to columns & columns to rows. It lets you arrange your data through any field (cell) and do computational power. More detailed data may be found in a variety of sources on the internet, such as. On the other hand, quite an answer may generate more problems than it resolves. There are other practical considerations as well.

What are some instances of Pivot Tables in training?

Create a list of different characteristics using a pivot table. Pivot tables may be employed to determine distinct values in a user table since they condense data. It is a simple method to examine all the values in a field and discover errors and other irregularities.

A pivot table may organize items/records/rows into sections, count the number of pieces in each category, total the items' values or calculate the average, identify the minimum or

maximum value, and so on. We'll see how graphs and charts work in just a few simple steps. Then developing pivot tables will no longer be difficult. Let's have a look at an example. Something will employ that we're all familiar with.

6.3 The Standard deck of 52-cards

Every card does have an icon (clubs, diamonds, hearts, spades), a value (A, 1 to several 10, J, Q, K), and a color (red, green, or blue) (black or red).

Let's group the deck by color:

black	
red	

The cards have been divided between two groups or 2 additional decks. What kind of data can we get from this table? For instance, we may count the decks in each of the groups.

Instead of collecting all of the decks in a single table, we may have the computer do it. As a consequence, all we perceive is a number. We also understand that the regular 52-card deck has an equal amount of black and red cards.

The designations black and red may be seen in the first line. Row Flags are what they're called. Isn't it a little disconcerting? Is it possible to have row labels inside a column? Yes, since each row need a label at the start. As a result, the labels are stacked one on top of the other, forming a column. Don't be perplexed by this. The row commences with a Row Label. What about if you flipped the board 90 degrees in the other direction?

Isn't there much that's changed? It does provide us with the same data. It is simply a matter of preference as to which form we tend to favor. One different thing would be that Row Labels are no longer used. Column Labels are used instead.

The colors red & black are still used in column labels. It is why they've branded each of the columns now. Column Labels, like Row Labels, are located at the start of the columns and eventuate to be side by side, starting to form a row. Look at the Pivot Table areas chart on Excel Campus for a better understanding.

Adding another dimension

Which other classifications does the standard 52-card deck have besides colors? There are icons (clubs, diamonds, hearts,

and spades, for instance). As a result, we could sort into categories based on the symbol.

clubs ♣	
diamonds ♦	
hearts ♥	
spades ♠	

Once more, we can ask the computer to sum up the cards for us.

How about if we wished to categorize the cards based on even more their characteristics (or attributes)? Let's incorporate the two approaches. Another component will be added to represent the color. The card figures now represent row Labels. The color will be added as Column Labels.

	red	black
clubs ♣		⬚⬚⬚⬚⬚⬚⬚⬚⬚⬚⬚⬚
diamonds ♦	⬚⬚⬚⬚⬚⬚⬚⬚⬚⬚⬚⬚	
hearts ♥	⬚⬚⬚⬚⬚⬚⬚⬚⬚⬚⬚⬚	
spades ♠		⬚⬚⬚⬚⬚⬚⬚⬚⬚⬚⬚⬚

Read the results

There are classifications because there are no cards, as you'll see. It has already revealed some valuable information. The table informs us that there were no red clubs, black diamonds, black hearts, or red spade if it was not for the cards we're all associated with. In these other sayings, clubs and spades are indeed black, while diamonds and hearts are still red. It's the first time we've used the pivot table in practice.

Rotation, juggling and more

Let's try the cards into their matters again. Let's look at several other ways to use the Row and Column Tags. It gives the same quality and data as before. It all varies depending on what better represents the narrative we're trying to tell.

- Rotation

- Multi-stage Row Labels

- Multi-stage Column Labels

The 2nd and 3rd situations seem to be a little more challenging. Explore how we may split the cards into groups based on their hue. Following that, we start dividing the cards into 4 categories based on the symbol.

We may also change the order in which the Column or Row Tags appear. Consider the following situation:

clubs ♣		diamonds ♦		hearts ♥		spades ♠	
red	black	red	black	red	black	red	black
	13	13		13			13

What a divide in the groups is not particularly practicable in a normal 52-card deck situation. As a result, many table cells stay unfilled. Many tools just pass over empty cells for the sake of simplicity. The output is more compact and simpler to read when the cells are skipped.

Sums and percentages

Counting the overall numbers in rows and columns can occasionally provide additional useful information. In the instance of the cards, certainly not. However, have a look. There

are indeed 26 red cards, 26 black cards, and 13 cards to each of the marks, as seen. It's vital to note that both Column Totals and Row Totals count exactly 52 cards. Even though columns and rows reflect multiple kinds of classifications, this is the case.

Have you taken note of how lovely the pivot table is? Its pivot table's cells are being used to split all the cards. Each card is only ever depicted once. It is like the actual world, in which a single card cannot be inserted into multiple decks at the same moment. We may be more concerned about relative worth. How much of the whole number is represented by each column or row? Half-way of the decks were red, and others were black. A third of all cards are used to represent particular symbols.

Let's pivot and get some pizza

We already understand how to identify the cards and place them in a pivot table. Let's look at an example that is a little more difficult. Our preferred establishment has given us a receipt. It looks a little like a card. It differs from the former in that it has additional qualities. A receipt is devoid of symbols and color. A receipt, on the other hand, has many new attributes. Its value (whole) stayed the same but with a new connotation.

What are some additional unique features of a receipt? These are the following:

Employee servicing the table event time and date goods sold (for example, pizza Margarita) price, taxes, total. There are numerous other characteristics on the receipt, such as the restaurant's phone number and address, station number, guest number, table number, etc. However, we will ignore those new properties because they are unimportant in our examples for the time being. Also, for simplicity, we'll assume that each invoice always contains only one product sold.

Tabularize the universe

A systematic form of Data is required for the desktop to work effectively with data. Therefore, we use tables to organize our characterizations of the world surrounding us. A single record in the table generally describes one item in the actual world. These could be components in a recipe, models of cars, or tasks to be completed. If we wished to tabularize our basic 52-card deck, we'd need a desk with 52 rows. Each row represents a single card. Anything along these lines: Place the pizza receipt on the table. Just the characteristics marked in red would be tracked.

Questions to answer

Do you have any suggestions for questions to ask regarding our pizza bills? What kind of information would we be able to obtain?

- How many pizzas were sold by whom?

- How many pizzas were sold of which type?

- Who brought in the most money (overall value of pizzas did sell)?

- Which pizzas brought in the most money?

Answers to these questions can assist us in selecting which pizza flavors to discontinue and which flavors to market more aggressively.

It might also assist us in determining staff incentives.

There are more difficult questions to respond to:

- What are the most popular pizzas in a particular month or season?

- Which kind of pizzas sells best in the morning and early afternoon?

6.4 Pizza Pivots

Let's take each question one at a time and try to answer it. Before we do that, there's one more phrase to learn about: Summation Values. The values from our main table used to create the Pivot Table's resultant value are Summation Values.

For example, in the case of a regular 52-card deck, we could utilize any characteristic of the cards because we were merely counting them. Counting the amounts of information is a simple procedure. We might also count the number of distinct values. We might also calculate the Total, average, minimum, maximum, and median... Almost everything is possible. Calculations typically operate on numeric fields with a few exceptions, such as count.

Who sold how many pizzas?

The employee is the row label. The Summation Values can be anything, including the Name of the Pizza.

Employee	Pizzas Count
Melissa	4
Sylvia	5
Juliette	4

We choose a limited number of entries (e.g., Receipt = pizzas sold). As a result, the outcomes are unsurprising.

Which type of Pizza was sold how many times?

Pizza is the Row Label. The Summation Values can be anything, including the Name of the Pizza.

Who generated what revenue (total value of pizzas sold)?

The employee is the row label. The sum of a Total column, the Summation Value, is now crucial. As you can see, we supply the column name and the calculation type for summation (i.e., sum).

Employee	Sum of Total
Melissa	$26.23
Sylvia	$33.16
Juliette	$25.53

It is becoming very intriguing. A Table with Subtotal is a term used to describe such a Pivot Table.

What Pizza generated what revenue?

Pizza is the Row Label. The total of a Total column remains the Summation Value. A column summary can also be included.

Pizza	Sum of Total
Margherita	$18.09
Quattro Stagioni	$26.96
Salami	$19.14
Tuna	$20.73
Grand Total	**$84.92**

We can see that we sold $84.92 worth of pizzas for the restricted quantity of receipts. Quattro Stagioni is the Pizza that brings in the most money.

Let's try it again using relative prices (i.e., percentages).

Pizza	% of Total
Margherita	21.30%
Quattro Stagioni	31.75%

Salami	22.54%
Tuna	24.41%
Grand Total	**100%**

6.5 Advanced Pizza Pivots

You're becoming a pro. Congratulations. Now we'll go into the more in-depth inquiries concerning our pizza receipts. We humans have an inherent ability to operate with time. We can identify whatever year or Month a date is when we see it.

It isn't true of all software applications. Some tools naturally grasp date and time (such as Lumber: Visual and simple project and team management) and require assistance.

If you have a tool that requires some assistance, make a new field with such a function that extracts the Month from the Date field (for example, retrieving the month numbers 05 from 2019/05/26 01:17 PM).

What type of pizzas are sold most in the given Month?

We've set both the Row Label (Pizza) and the Column Labels this time.

Pizza / Month	May	June	July
Margherita	1	2	0
Quattro Stagioni	1	1	2
Salami	1	1	1
Tuna	1	1	1

What kinds of pizzas are more popular in the morning or afternoon?

Pizza / Time	1PM	2PM	3PM
Margherita	1	1	1
Quattro Stagioni	1	1	2
Salami	0	2	1
Tuna	0	1	2

We only have afternoon sales data, and we can at least track sales by an hour of the day. We'll add another layer of Row Label for the most complicated example.

Let's take a look at who sold the most pizzas each Month. The employee is the first-row label; Pizza is the second-row label; Month (from the Date / Time column) is the Column Label, and the Summation Numbers are counted.

Employee	Pizza / Month	May	June	July
Melissa	Margherita	1	0	0
	Quattro Stagioni	0	0	0
	Salami	0	1	0
	Tuna	1	0	1
Sylvia	Margherita	0	1	0
	Quattro Stagioni	1	0	2
	Salami	0	0	0
	Tuna	0	1	0
Juliette	Margherita	0	1	0
	Quattro Stagioni	0	1	0
	Salami	1	0	1
	Tuna	0	0	0

We can't tell anything from the outcome because of our limited data collection. Maybe we didn't check one final item- is there somebody specializing in selling a certain pizza? How would you use a Pivot Table to address such a question? Let's use Employees as that of the Row Label & Pizza as even the Column Label to see what we can come up with.

Employee / Pizza	Margherita	Quattro Stagioni	Salami	Tuna
Melissa	1	0	1	2
Sylvia	1	3	0	1
Juliette	1	1	2	0

Sylvia is unquestionably our Quattro Stagioni guru. However, we might consider the value it provides to us.

Employ-ee / Pizza	Margher-ita	Quat-tro Sta-gioni	Sala-mi	Tuna	Grand Total
Melissa	$6.03	0	$6.38	$13.82	$26.23
Sylvia	$6.03	$20.22	0	$6.91	$33.16
Juliette	$6.03	$6.74	$12.76	0	$25.53
Grand Total	$18.09	$26.96	$19.14	$20.73	$84.92

We can now see that Sylvia is not just an expert at selling Quattro Stagioni but also at bringing in the most money for the organization.

Ordering, sorting, A-Z...

Searching for high values in the resultant Pivot Table is handy. Manually scrolling through the database, especially if it is vast,

is time-consuming, mistake-prone, and does not effectively express your story.

Fortunately, we can use the computer to sort the rows and columns. The rows and columns may both be sorted. What criteria do we use to categorize them?

The data blocks can be sorted by respective Labels (Row Labels & Column Labels). It might be sorted alphabetically, in temporal order (for example, when using months as just a label), or in value order.

Employee / Pizza	Margherita	Quattro Stagioni	Salami	Tuna	Grand Total
Juliette	$6.03	$6.74	$12.76	0	$25.53
Melissa	$6.03	0	$6.38	$13.82	$26.23
Sylvia	$6.03	$20.22	0	$6.91	$33.16
Grand Total	$18.09	$26.96	$19.14	$20.73	$84.92

The rows can then be sorted by value in several columns, or values can sort the columns in several rows. Some of the rows' values can be used to order the columns.

Employee / Pizza	Quattro Stagioni	Margherita	Salami	Tuna	Grand Total
Sylvia	$20.22	$6.03	0	$6.91	$33.16
Melissa	0	$6.03	$6.38	$13.82	$26.23
Juliette	$6.74	$6.03	$12.76	0	$25.53
Grand Total	$26.96	$18.09	$19.14	$20.73	$84.92

The Grand Total row and column can also sort the data blocks.

That effectively confines us to only one order per direction (vertically & horizontally). We can occasionally set sub-orders when some of the sorted values are equal.

Let's have a check at an illustration. We will sort the preceding Pivot Table horizontally (←→) by Grand Total rows and vertically (↑↓) even by Grand Total columns.

Employee / Pizza	Margherita	Salami	Tuna	Quattro Stagioni	Grand Total
Juliette	$6.03	$12.76	0	$6.74	**$25.53**
Melissa	$6.03	$6.38	$13.82	0	**$26.23**
Sylvia	$6.03	0	$6.91	$20.22	**$33.16**
Grand Total	**$18.09**	**$19.14**	**$20.73**	**$26.96**	**$84.92**

The numbers in Grand Total rows and the Grand Total columns are sorted, as can be seen. We can also see that our most popular Pizza is Quattro Stagioni, and that Sylvia is the employee with the highest revenue.

In Pivot Tables, we frequently reverse the sorting order so that the largest values appear first.

Employ-ee / Pizza	Quat-tro Sta-gioni	Tuna	Sala-mi	Margher-ita	Grand Total
Sylvia	$20.22	$6.91	0	$6.03	$33.16
Melissa	0	$13.82	$6.38	$6.03	$26.23
Juliette	$6.74	0	$12.76	$6.03	$25.53
Grand Total	$26.96	$20.73	$19.14	$18.09	$84.92

We could, for example, sort by employee name. However, in this case, any subsequent sorting would invalidate the earlier sorting.

Is it possible to utilize several sorting orders? Yes, it is when there are many labels in a row or column.

We may think of having several Row Labels as having multiple independent tables.

Melissa:

Pizza / Month	May	June	July
Margherita	1	0	0
Quattro Stagioni	0	0	0
Salami	0	1	0
Tuna	1	0	1

Sylvia:

Pizza / Month	May	June	July
Margherita	0	1	0
Quattro Stagioni	1	0	2
Salami	0	0	0
Tuna	0	1	0

The "inner" tables can be sorted the same way as the "outer" tables. Furthermore, the total order of those tables may be sorted.

For example, we may arrange them by employee name.

Employee, Pizza, and Month are sorted in this Pivot Table.

Juliette:

Pizza / Month	May	June	July
Margherita	0	1	0
Quattro Stagioni	0	1	0
Salami	1	0	1
Tuna	0	0	0

Is there anything (aside from the Employee name) that could affect the order of the inner tables? Yes, it is. To each inner table, we'll add total counts.

Employee	Pizza / Month	May	June	July	Grand Total
Juliette	Margherita	0	1	0	1
	Quattro Stagioni	0	1	0	1
	Salami	1	0	1	2
	Tuna	0	0	0	0
	Total	1	2	1	4
Melissa	Margherita	1	0	0	1
	Quattro Stagioni	0	0	0	0
	Salami	0	1	0	1
	Tuna	1	0	1	2
	Total	2	1	1	4

	Margherita	0	1	0	1
	Quattro Sta-gioni	1	0	2	3
Sylvia	Salami	0	0	0	0
	Tuna	0	1	0	1
	Total	1	2	2	5
Grand Total		4	5	4	13

Apart from maintaining the order of the inner tables (Pizza name & Month), we have had the following alternatives for sorting them:

- Name of the employee (marked in light blue)
- Total sales in May, June, or July.
- Sales totals for each inner table

Of course, the same idea may be used in several Column Labels.

6.6 Filtering

When it comes to Pivot Tables, the last jigsaw piece that is sometimes overlooked is filtering. Filtering is just the process of removing several of the data row (a record) from the source database.

In the resultant Pivot Table, just the values that may pass filters are kept. The filters usually compare values to a constant (for example, Receipt Total $6.50) or check for the presence of a value in a range or a list. Filtering works with the data sources and just affects the input for Pivot Table, which is a bit surprising. Filters do not affect the Pivot Table. That is how it works:

Rows from the source table -> Filters -> Values from the source table that passed the filter -> Pivot Table

6.7 Pivot Tables in various tools

We've been discussing in broad terms thus far, with no particular device in mind. You may apply your new skills to any program your firm uses, including Libre Office, Open Office, Microsoft Office, Google Sheets, and many more.

Let's look at how the Table settings in the most common tools appear so you can get comfortable with them and start using them right away. We utilized the same pizza sales data as in prior examples for all of the tools.

The objective is to build the sophisticated Pivot Table containing employees, Pizza, and month-by-month pizza sales. The employee is the first Row Label; Pizza is the second Row Label; the Month is the Column Label (as from the Date and Time column), and the Summation Value is counted.

How do you create a Pivot Table?

To construct a Pivot Table in most tools, just highlight desired sheet region and choose a function (usually in the Data menu). Take a couple of examples using Microsoft Office as an example. Ideas is a tool in Microsoft Office that may even propose some simple Pivot Tables depending on the current sheet. It might be an excellent start to work it.

Microsoft Office 365

We had to add a column with the month number because Excel didn't learn how to control date and time by default. We will not go into depth on how to compute its month number from a date because it is not a simple procedure. Although the end

product isn't really "appealing," it was enough to seek Pivot Table in the Ideas area and add further fields.

Row Labels are placed under Rows, Columns Label is placed under Columns, & Summation Values are placed under Values. Fields refer to the names of the columns.

Additional options, such as sorting, displaying data, and using grand totals, are available via context menus adjacent to each field. The user interfaces of the other Office versions are largely the same.

Google Sheets

Due to Google Sheets' inability to parse dates natively, an extra table column containing the Month values was required. The output, on the other hand, is a little prettier.

The terms used in the settings are the same as in Microsoft Excel. Summation Values are Values, Row Label is Row, Column Label is Column, and Row Labels are Columns. Predefined themes, which can be swapped with a button press and give the entire Pivot Table a new appearance and feel, are a great feature of Google Sheets.

6.8 LibreOffice Calc

We had to construct a distinct Month column since LibreOffice does not recognize the time and date field on its own. It comes as no surprise. The end outcome is unsatisfactory. It requires considerable manual adjusting to achieve a pleasing appearance.

	A	B	C	D	E	F
1	Count - Pizza		Month ▾			
2	Employee ▾	Pizza ▾	05	06	07	Total Result
3	Juliette	Margharita		1		1
4		Quattro Stagioni		1		1
5		Salami	1		1	2
6	Melissa	Margharita	1			1
7		Salami		1		1
8		Tuna	1		1	2
9	Sylvia	Margharita		1		1
10		Quattro Stagi▸	1		2	3
11		Tuna		1		1
12	Total Result		4	5	4	13

The Pivot Table settings in LibreOffice are the most perplexing we've encountered, and the vocabulary is different from that of other tools. Row Labels are referred to as Row fields, Column Labels are referred to as Column fields, & Summation Values are referred to as Data Fields. More individual field settings are concealed — double-clicking on individual fields opens a new window with even more options.

Apple Numbers

Even though Apple Number is a spreadsheets editor, it lacks a Pivot Table feature. Although there are workarounds for simulating simple Pivot Tables, this is not a table service calculator.

Lumber

Lumber seems to be the only application that understands time and date by default. We didn't need to add a customized Month column for the first time. Every table in Lumber has its Symbol and color, and the output look and feel takes this into account.

According to conventional nomenclature, row Labels are rows, Column Labels are Columns, and Summation Values are Values. The values of all settings are instantly visible and accessible.

CHAPTER 7: CONDITIONAL FORMATTING IN EXCEL

7.1 Quickly Identify Duplicates

In Excel, conditional formatting may be used to find duplicates in a dataset.

Here's how to go about it:

- Choose the dataset wherein you wish to see duplicates highlighted.

- Select Home –> Conditional Formatting –> Underlining Cell Regulations –> Duplicate Values from the menu bar at the top of the screen.

- Ensure Duplicate is chosen inside the left dropdown inside the Duplicate Value dialogue box. By using the right dropdown, you can select the format for use. You can select one of the pre-existing formats or create your own using the Custom Format option.

- Click OK.

That Would show all the cells in the specified data set with a duplication. A single column, many columns, or a non-contiguous group of cells can all be used to store your data.

7.2 Underscore Cells with Value Bigger/Less than a Total

In Excel, conditional formatting may rapidly highlight cells with values greater or less than a certain threshold. For example, any cells having a sales value of less than $100 million should be highlighted, as should any cells with a mark below the passing level.

The following are the measures to take:

- Choose the entire dataset.

- Select Home -> Conditional Formatting -> Highlight Cell Rules -> Bigger Than / Less Than.

- A dialogue box will appear depending on your choice (more than or less than). Assume you've chosen the 'Greater than' option. Enter a number in the left-hand area of the dialogue box. The goal is to draw attention to cells with a value larger than the given value.

- Using the right-hand dropdown, specify the formatting applied to the fields that fulfill the requirement. You can select one of the pre-existing formats or create your own using the Custom Format option.

- Click OK.

That would highlight all cells in a dataset with values exceeding 5 instantly.

Note: If you want to emphasize numbers more than or equal to 5, use conditional formatting using the "Equal To" requirement.

Repeat the process to highlight fields with a value just over a specific value.

7.3 Highlighting Top/Bottom 10 (or 10%)

Excel's conditional formatting can easily determine the top 10 items or the top 10% of a data collection. That might be useful in cases where you need to view the top applicants based on their scores or the top deal value in the sales figures rapidly.

Similarly, you may easily discover the worst 10 entries in a dataset or the bottom 10%.

The following are the measures to take:

- Choose the complete dataset from the dropdown menu.

- Select Home -> Conditional Formatting -> Top/Bottom Rules -> Top 10 Items (or percent) / Bottom 10 Items from the drop-down menu (or percent).

- The dialogue box will open depending on what you pick. If you choose the Top 10 things, a dialogue window will appear, as seen below:

- Using the right-hand dropdown, select the format that will be applied to the fields that fulfill the requirement. You can select one of the pre-existing formats or utilize the Custom Format options to create your own.

- Click OK.

That would showcase the top ten things in the specified dataset right away. It's worth noting that this only works for fields with a number value. Also, all cells will be highlighted if the dataset has less than 10 cells and you choose to highlight the Top ten items/ Bottom 10 Items.

7.4 Highlighting Errors/Blanks

If you deal with various numerical data & calculations in Excel, you know how critical it is to recognize and address cells that contain mistakes or are blank. If all these cells are utilized in subsequent calculations, the results may be incorrect.

In Excel, conditional formatting can assist you in swiftly identifying and highlighting cells that contain mistakes or are blank.

Assume we have the following dataset:

There is a blank cell (A4) in this data collection and mistakes (A5 and A6).

Steps:

- Choose the dataset you wish to see blank cells and cells with mistakes highlighted.

- Select Home –> Conditional Formatting –> New Rule from the dropdown menu.

- Select New Formatting Rule in this New Format Rule dialogue icon. To identify which cells to format, use a formula.

- In the 'Edit the Rule Description' section, type =OR(IS-BLANK(A1). ISERROR(A1)) in the formula box.

- The algorithm above examines all cells for two conditions: whether they are blank or not and if they have an error. It returns whether any of the criteria are TRUE.

- Select the format you wish to use for blank cells or contain mistakes. To do so, go to the Format menu and choose format. It will bring up the 'Formatting Cells' dialogue icon, where you might choose your format.

- Click OK.

That will highlight all of the cells which are either empty or contain mistakes.

You don't have to utilize the complete range A1:A7 in the calculation in conditional formatting. Only A1 is used in the formula above. Excel checks one line at a time and updates the reference when you apply this formula to the full range. When it tests A1, for example, it applies the formula =OR(ISBLANK(A1), ISERROR(A1)). It then uses the algorithm =OR(BLANK (A2), ERROR(A2)) to examine cell A2. Depending on which cell is being evaluated, it automatically updates the reference (since they are relative references). As a result, you won't have to create a formula for every cell. Excel can change this cell reference on its own.

7.5 Creating Heat Maps

A heat map is a data visualization in which the color symbolizes the value of a cell. You may, for example, make a heat map in which the cell with the greatest value is colored green, and the color shifts to red as the value drops.

As illustrated in the example below:

The numbers in the above data set range from 1 to 100. The value in a cell is used to highlight it. The green color is assigned to 100 people, whereas the red color is assigned to one person.

Here are the instructions for making heat maps in Excel using Conditional Formatting.

- Choose a data set.

- Select one of the color schemes from Home –> Conditional Formatting –> Color Scales.

The heatmap icon will apply the format to the dataset as simply click it. You have a variety of color gradients to pick from. If the available color selections do not satisfy you, you may add more rules and define the color you desire. You may also use Data Bard & Icon sets in the same way.

7.6 Highlight Every Other Row/Column

To make the data more readable, you might wish to highlight alternate rows.

These are known as zebra lines, and they may be especially useful for printing data.

These zebra lines may now be made in two ways. Converting your tabular data into such an Excel Table is the quickest method. It added color to alternate rows automatically. You may learn more about it by clicking here.

Conditional formatting is another option.

Assume you have the following dataset:

Here's how to use conditional formatting in Excel to highlight alternate rows.

- Choose a dataset. Select A2:C13 in the example above (which excludes the header). Select the whole data set if you wish to include the header.

- Go to Home-> Conditional Formatting-> New Rule to open the Conditional Formatting dialogue box. [Alt + O] is a keyboard shortcut.

- Select 'Use a Formula to Determine Which Cells' in the dialogue box.

- In the 'Edit the Rule Description' section, type =ISODD(ROW()) in the formula box.

- The preceding algorithm scans all cells and returns TRUE if the ROW number is odd. The conditional format supplied would be applied to all cells that return TRUE.

- Choose a format for the cells that are blank or contain mistakes. To do so, go to the Format menu and select format from the dropdown menu. It'll bring up the 'Formatting Cells' dialogue icon, where you may choose the format.

- Click OK.

That concludes our discussion. The data set's alternative rows will be highlighted.

In many circumstances, the same strategy may be used. All you have to do is utilize the appropriate conditional formatting formula. Some instances are as follows:

- Draw attention to alternating even rows: =ISEVEN(ROW())

- Use =ISODD(ROW()) to highlight alternate add rows.

- Every third row is highlighted: =MOD(ROW(),3)=0

7.7 Search and Highlight Data using Conditional Formatting

It is a more advanced application of conditional formatting. It really would make you appear like a rockstar in Excel. Assume you have such a dataset with the following columns: Product Name, Sales Rep, & Geography. The aim is to write a string in cell C2, and have it highlighted if it matches any other cell(s) data.

The steps to develop this Search and Highlight capability are as follows:

- Choose a dataset.

- Go to Home –> Conditional Formatting -> New Rule (Alt + D + O is a keyboard shortcut).

- Choose the option 'Use the formula to verify which sections to format' in the New Formatting Rule dialogue box.

- In the 'Edit the Rule Description' box, enter the following formula: =AND($C$2>"",$C$2=B5)

- Select the format you wish to use for blank cells or contain mistakes. To do so, go to the Format menu and choose format. It will bring up the 'Formatting Cells' dialogue icon, where you may choose your format.

- Click OK.

That concludes our discussion. When you type something in cell C2 and press enter, it will highlight all the cells that match.

How does this work?

The conditional formatting formula assesses all of the cells within the dataset. Assume you arrive in Japan in cell C2. Excel would now analyze each cell's calculation. When two requirements are satisfied, the formula returns TRUE for a cell:

Cell C2 is not empty, and its contents are identical to those of the cells in the dataset. As a result, all cells containing the text Japan are highlighted.

How to Remove Conditional Formatting in Excel

Unless you delete conditional formatting explicitly, it stays in place once it's been applied. Keep conditional formatting applied solely to the cells where you need it as a wise practice. It may cause a sluggish Excel worksheet since it is volatile.

Select the cells you wish to get rid of it from to get rid of conditional formatting.

- Select Home –> Conditional Formatting –> Then Clear Rules –> Then Clear Rules from Chosen Cells from the dropdown menu.

- Select Clear Rules from Entire Sheet to eliminate conditional formatting from the entire worksheet.

Important things to know about Conditional Formatting in MS Excel

- Conditional formatting is unstable. It may result in a sluggish worksheet. Only use it when necessary.

- When you copy and paste cells with conditional formatting, the conditional formatting is copied.

- All rules stay active if you apply several rules to the same group of cells. In the event of a conflict, the rule applied last takes precedence. You may, however, alter the order using the Manage Rules dialogue box.

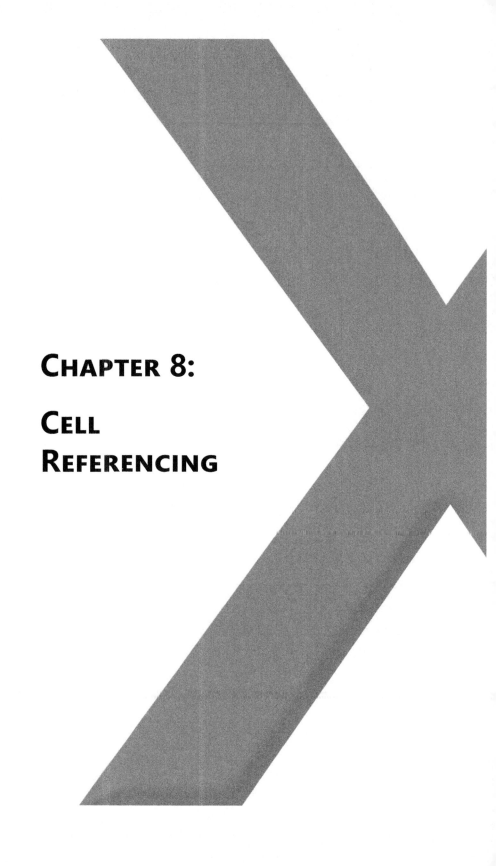

CHAPTER 8:

CELL
REFERENCING

8.1 What is a cell reference in Excel?

A cell reference, also known as a cell address, is a formula that specifies a cell on a worksheet by combining a column letter with a row number. A1 indicates the cell at the intersection of column A & row 1; B2 indicates the second cell in the column B; & so on.

Cell referencing is used in formulas to assist Excel in discovering the numbers that the calculation should compute. To copy the values of A1 to some other cell, for example, use the following formula: =A1. You may use this formula to sum the numbers in cells A1 and A2: =A1+A2.

8.2 What is a range reference in Excel?

A range in Microsoft Excel is a group of 2 or more cells. A range of references is formed by separating the addresses of the top left and bottom-right cells by a colon. The range A1:C2, for example, has 6 cells numbered A1 through C2.

Excel reference styles

In Excel, there are two address styles: A1 and R1C1.

A1 reference style in Excel

Most of the time, A1 seems to be the default style. Columns are specified by letters, and numbers in this format define rows. Thus A1 identifies a cell in column A, row 1.

R1C1 reference type in MS Excel

The R1C1 style uses numerals to identify both rows and columns, i.e., A cell in row 1, column 1 is designated as R1C1. Both A1 & R1C1 reference styles are shown in the screenshot below:

Select file> Then Options > Then Formulas, then unmark the R1C1 reference type box to convert from the default A1 style to R1C1.

How to create a reference in Excel

To create a cell reference on the same sheet, follow these steps:

- Select the cell where the formula should be entered.

- Type the equal Symbol (=) in the box.

- Select one of the following options:

- Directly type the reference in the cell or the formula bar, or o Click the cell you wish to refer to.

- Finish the formula by typing the remainder of it and pressing the Enter key.

To add the numbers in cells A1 & A2, for example, type equal, click A1, type plus, click A2, and then press Enter. Choose a range of cells on the worksheet to create a range reference. To add the values in cells A1, A2, and A3, for example, type equal followed by the Name of the SUM function as well as the opening brackets, select cells A1 across A3, type the closing brackets, & press Enter:

Accordingly, select the row number/column letter to refer to the complete row or column. To include all the cells in row 1, for example, start entering the SUM function and then click the first row's header to include the row reference in your formula:

How to change Excel cell reference in a formula

Follow these procedures to update a cell address inside an existing formula:

- Double-click the cell that contains the formula & press F2 to enter Edit mode, or click the cell and press F2. Each cell/ range addressed by the formula will be highlighted in a distinct color.

To alter a mobile phone's address, use one of the following methods:

- Remove the reference from the formula and replace it with a new one.

- Choose a cell or range on the sheet, then choose the references in the formula.

- Drag the cell or range's color-coded boundary to include more or fewer cells in a reference.

- Press the Enter key on your keyboard.

How to cross-reference in Excel

To reference cells in a separate worksheet or Excel file, you must first specify the target cell(s) and the sheet & Workbook where they are situated. It can be accomplished by employing a technique known as an external cell reference.

How to reference another sheet in Excel

Type the Name of the destination worksheet preceded by such an exclamation point (.) even before the cell or range address to refer to a cell or range of cells in another worksheet. Here's an example of referring to cell A1 on Sheet 2 in the same Workbook: =Sheet2.A1

If the worksheet's Name contains spaces or non-alphabetic characters, it must be enclosed in single quote marks, for example: ='Target sheet.'A1

You may have Excel establish external references for you directly to avoid typos and mistakes. Here's how to do it:

- In a cell, begin entering a formula.

- Select the cell/range of cells you wish to cross-reference by clicking the sheet tab users would like to cross-reference.

- When you've finished inputting your formula, press Enter.

How to reference another workbook in Excel

You must provide the workbook name in brackets, next to the sheet name, exclamation mark, and the cell or range address in a separate Excel file to refer to a range of cells. Consider the following scenario: =[Book1.xlsx]Sheet1.A1

If the file/sheet name contains non-alphabetic characters, use single quotation marks to encapsulate the path, e.g., ='[Target file. xlsx]Sheet1'.A1

8.3 Relative, absolute, & mixed cell references

There are 3 various cell references in MS Excel: relative, absolute, & mixed. You can use any formula when composing a formula for a single cell. However, suppose you want to transfer your formula to certain other cells. The correct address type would be best, as absolute and relative cell references act when copied to other cells.

Relative cell reference in Excel

A relative reference is one in which the row or column coordinates do not include the $ sign, such as A1 or A1:B10. Excel's cell addresses are all relative by default.

When rows and columns are changed or duplicated across many cells, relative references change. You must utilize relative cell references to repeat the same computation over several columns or rows.

To multiply integers in column A by 5, put the following formula in B2: =A2*5. The formula will change when transferred from row 2 to row 3: =A3*5.

Absolute cell reference in Excel

The dollar symbol ($) in the column or row coordinate indicates an absolute reference, such as $A$1 or $A$1:$B$10. An exact cell reference remains unchanged when filling additional cells with the same formula. When you need to do many computations with a number in a single cell or replicate a formula to additional cells without altering references, absolute addresses come in handy.

To multiply the numbers in column A by the number in column B2, for example, type the following formula in row 2 and then drag the fill handle down the column to replicate the formula:

=A2*$B$2. The relative reference (A2) will vary depending on the relative location of the row where the formula is duplicated; however, the absolute reference ($B$2) will never change:

Mixed cell reference

A mixed reference, such as $A1 or A$1, has one absolute and one relative coordinate. Many instances exist where just one coordinate, row or column, has to be corrected. To multiply a column of integers (column A) by three separate numbers (B2, C2, and D2), for example, enter the following formula in B3 and duplicate it down and to the right: =$A3*B$2.

Since the formula should always multiply the original numbers in column A, you lock the column coordinate in $A3. Because it must change for additional rows, the row coordinates are relative. To instruct Excel to always choose the multiplier in row 2, you lock the row coordinates in B$2. Because the multiplier is in three distinct columns, the column coordinates are relative, and the formula should change accordingly. As a consequence, all of the computations are done using a single formula that changes for each row or column it is copied to:

How to switch between different reference types

You may manually type or erase the $ sign to go from a relative to an absolute reference, or you can use the F4 shortcut:

- Select the formula-containing cell by double-clicking it.
- Choose the reference you wish to alter from the dropdown menu.
- Toggle between four reference types by pressing F4.

By repeatedly pressing the F4 key, the references are switched in the following order: A1 > $A$1 > A$1 > $A1.

8.4 Circular reference in Excel

A circular reference, in basic words, refers to its cell, either directly or indirectly. If you write the following formula in cell A1, for example, you'll get a circular reference: =A1+100

Circular references are troublesome in most instances, and you should avoid them wherever feasible. However, they may be the sole viable option for a given task in certain rare cases.

3D reference in Excel

The same cell or set of cells on many worksheets is a 3-D reference. For example, you may use the AVERAGE function with a 3d reference to find the average values in cells A1 through A10 on Sheets 1, 2, and 3. =AVERAGE(Sheet1:Sheet3.A1:A3)

Here's how to build a formula with such a three-dimensional reference:

- As usual, begin entering a formula in a cell; in this case, we type =AVERAGE(

- To include the first sheet in the 3d reference, click the first sheet tab.

- While holding down the Shift key, click the final sheet's tab.

- Decide the cell (or range of cells) you want to compute.

- When you've finished inputting the formula, press the Enter key to finish it.

Excel structured reference (table references)

Structured reference is a phrase for using table & column names instead of cell addresses in a calculation. Such references may only be used in Excel tables to refer to cells. For example, this method may be used to get the average of figures in Table1's Sales column:

=AVERAGE(Table1[Sales])

Excel names (named range)

In Excel, you can also declare a cell or a group of cells by Name. Simply choose a cell or cells, put a name in the Name Box, then click the Enter key.

Once you've created new names, you may want to update the old cell reference in your formulae with the defined Name. Here's how to do it:

- Select the formula cells you want to replace cell references with names.

- Select any blank cell on the current sheet to replace all references with specified names in all formulae.

- Click the arrow next to Define Name, then click Apply Names... under the Formulas tab > Defined Names group.

- Select one or more names in the Apply Names dialogue box, then click OK.

As a consequence, all or chosen formula references will be modified to the relevant names.

CHAPTER 9:

TIPS AND TRICKS

9.1 6 Super Cool Excel Tips & Tricks For Beginners

It would be beneficial if you had quick solutions and procedures for conquering any obstacles you may have encountered. For you, there are some of the easiest, quickest, and most current options. Once you've mastered these, you'll find working with Excel sheets a lot of fun. Most importantly, you'll be able to put the following tips into practice without reading them again.

Using a shortcut key, choose rows and columns. Is it a waste of time to pick rows and columns? But wait, there's a way out. Simply press Shift + Space to select the full row. Ctrl + Space will select a column

How to Add signs with shortcut

- Use Ctrl + Shift +. to transpose a number with two decimal points.

- Press Ctrl + Shift + $ to get money.

- To calculate percentages, press Ctrl + Shift + percent.

How to Find data and replace it in excel

When working with a large amount of data, it might be difficult to locate a certain word or word in an excel sheet. The discover

feature can assist by searching the document for that word or phrase. Simply press Ctrl + F to launch a new window.

After that, input the words, and you can either search them one at a time or use the find all option. Then, select the Replace tab, type the word you wish to replace, and click OK. That's all there is to it.

136

How to add a strikethrough

When working with MS Excel, the strikethrough option indicates that a job has been finished or checked off.

- To add a strikethrough, press Ctrl+5 and choose the cell you wish to apply the strikethrough format to.

- If you try to apply the strikethrough to a group of cells, select all of them and use the same shortcut.

How to hide data from the worksheet

Select the cells in your excel sheet that you wish to conceal and follow the easy procedures. Right-click -> Format Cells -> Custom -> ;;; (Three semicolons).

Easy way to make a borderline of a selected cell

The quickest technique to make the boundaries of your cell is to use Excel shortcuts. Begin by using the following method: Press Ctrl+Shift+& choose the area you wish to border. Excel

Tricks and Tips for beginners have been finished, and now the semi-intermediate level will be discussed. There's a lot of information juice there.

9.2 7 Super Cool Excel Tips & Tricks For Semi-intermediates

The following Excel hints are for individuals who are still working with sheets but haven't done so in a long time. Saving time is simple for semi-intermediates since there are several strategies accessible. It is narrowed down to seven Cool Excel Tips & Tricks.

Easy way to insert a row and a column with a shortcut key

To make one row below, select an entire row & press Ctrl+Shift+ Plus(+). To delete a row, select it in its entirety. If you wish to remove many rows, hold down Ctrl and drag. Ctrl+Shift + Minus will erase the row (-). Keep in mind that this will remove any chosen rows.

Follow the same procedures as before to establish a new column. Ctrl+shift+Plus(+) to select the full column. A new column will be added to the right side of the screen. To eliminate a column, select the entire column & press Ctrl+Shift + Minus(-).

It's the quickest and most straightforward approach to creating rows and columns. Ctrl+shift+Plus(+) is a shortcut. A row and a column can be deleted using the same manner. Press the Ctrl+- Shift+Minus(-) key combination.

How to add the current date & time without typing

- Press Ctrl + to insert the current date into a cell. If you want to include the current time, use Ctrl+Shift+.

- Press Ctrl+Shift+# to change the date format. Similarly, Ctrl+- Shift+@ can be used to change the time format.

How to hide rows and columns with a shortcut key

- Select any cell in a row and press "Ctrl+9" to conceal it. Select any cell in a column and press "Ctrl+0" to make it invisible.

- Select several cells & press Ctrl+9 to hide columns and Ctrl+0 to conceal rows to hide multiple rows and columns.

A shortcut to the auto sum without typing or using a mouse

Normally, we choose the region and then use the auto sum function to determine the amount, or we use the formula to finish it. However, you may pick the region and press ALT+ Equal(=) to get a total sum or amount faster and easier.

Getting the average of numbers inserted in your cells

Are you attempting to calculate the average of the numbers in the cells? Simply plug in the formula =AVERAGE (Sell Range). Use the formula =SUM to add the numbers in a column (Sell Range).

Hyperlink a cell to a website

If you're utilizing Excel sheets for relevant social media stats, hyperlinking the cell might be useful. It allows you to have a reference column that lists all of the links each row is monitoring. When you add a URL to Excel directly, it must be clickable by default.

However, when it comes to hyperlink terms, such as the post's headline or the page title you're tracking, you should:

- Highlight the words you want to link to.

- Now hit Ctrl+K on your keyboard. A box will appear, allowing you to insert your linked URL.

- In that little box, copy and paste your URL. After that, press the enter key.

- For whatever reason, the shortcut does not always function. You may complete the operation manually by highlighting the cell and tapping > Hyperlink.

How can you turn text into columns?

Turning text into a column is one of the most popular Excel Tips & Tricks. You have a names-filled column that goes from first to last, and you're searching for two columns to separate them. Perform the following actions:

- Decide on the data first. Press the text to column option (at the extreme top).

- Now choose to separate them by a set width or delimiters (commas or spaces appropriate for CSV data values).

- When all of your data is crammed into the first column but divided by a set amount of periods and spaces, you utilize fixed-width.

- The rest is a little like magic, with additional options for specific numbers.

9.3 10 Super Cool Excel Tips & Tricks For Intermediates

A prepared collection of 9 techniques for the intermediates. Pushing your level higher while you're an intermediate Excel sheet operator isn't difficult. You'll become smarter after reading the following 9 fantastic tips.

How to Eliminate duplicate data sets or points

When working with bigger data sets, it's possible that duplicate data could appear, which can be time-consuming to eliminate manually. Frequently, you'll be given a list of several contacts, phone numbers, items, etc. In such cases, you hunt for a shortcut to eliminate the duplicates and create a flawless list with no repeated value.

- To eliminate all duplicates, choose the column/row where you wish to get rid of them.
- Now move to the Data icon & choose "Eliminate Duplicates" from the dropdown menu (in Tools).
- A confirmation pop-up would appear around the data you wish to work with.
- Select "Remove Duplicates," and that's all there is.

How to Transpose rows into columns

Let's simplify transposing row into the column as you move down the Excel Tips and Tricks list. When your spreadsheet has fewer data rows, we frequently need to convert the elements in one of those rows into columns.

Each header requires a lot of time to copy and paste. The transpose function is used in this case. It allows you to finish that operation by converting row data to columns.

- To transpose a column into rows, select it and highlight it.
- Select "Copy" from the right-click menu.
- Decide where your first row/column should begin on your sheet.
- Choose "Paste Special" after right-clicking the cell.

- A module will appear. There will be a transposition option accessible at the bottom.

- Finally, check that item and press OK.

- It will convert your columns to a row simply and efficiently.

How to add a checkbox in the Excel sheet

Are you wanting to monitor something that isn't measurable and is using an Excel sheet to manage consumer data? In this scenario, checkboxes should be added to a column.

Assume you're managing sales prospects with an Excel sheet, and you want to make sure you're keeping track of whether you phoned them in the previous quarter. In such instance, you may create a column named "Phoned this quarter?" and check off the cell in it when you've called the appropriate customer.

Let's have a look at how to accomplish it with Excel.

- In the spreadsheet, highlight a cell where you want to add checkboxes.

- Select DEVELOPER from the dropdown menu.

- Select the checkbox under FORM CONTROLS.

- Once the box is displayed in the cell, copy it.

- Highlight the cells where you want them to appear. Now you must paste it.

How to insert dropdown menus in MS Excel sheet

Are you using your spreadsheet for qualitative purposes, such as keeping track of things? It takes a long time to write the same terms over and over again, such as "Yes," "No," "Sales Lead," "Customer Stage," and so on. Dropdown menus are quite useful in this situation.

You can rapidly add notes to your contacts, items, services, or whatever else you're tracking. To add dropdowns to your cells, follow these steps:

- You want to place the dropdowns into those highlighted cells.

- Next, go to the top navigation and select the Data option.

- There will be a Data Validation Settings box available.

- Think about "Allow choices" and "Lists."

- Choose from a dropdown menu.

- After ticking the In-Cell dropdown box, press OK.

Dealing with Line Breaks and Wrapping Text

We all despise typing into spreadsheet cells since the default is for whatever you're typing to go on indefinitely without wrapping down to a new line. Surely, something can be done about that.

To start a new line, use Alt+Enter (using Enter as a single will exit the cell). Then select Wrap Text from the dropdown menu. It was under the Home tab at the top of the screen. When you choose to wrap text, all text will wrap around the cell's edge (the cell you're in). The text will re-wrap to fit when you resize the row/column.

Ctrl+Shift to Select:

Choosing a dataset is now significantly faster than moving the pointer with the mouse.

- Hold down Ctrl+Shift while slicking your first picked cell.

- You can obtain everything in the column above by pressing the UP arrow, or everything in the column below by pressing the DOWN arrow, or you can receive everything in the row by pressing the LEFT or RIGHT arrow (undoubtedly, to the left or right)

- Now combine the methods for acquiring a full column and everything in the row (available on the right/left).

- It will only choose cells that have data. If you press Ctrl+Shift+End, the cursor will go to the lowest cell (right-hand) with data and select everything in between.

As a result, if the arrow is in this A1 cell (high-left cell), that is it. Even better: pressing Ctrl+Shift+* (the asterisk) selects the whole data set, regardless of which cell is chosen.

How to autofill in Excel Sheets

However, it's a no-brainer. Even the intermediates are in charge of it. If you have a long day, you may relieve your boredom by typing a succession of repetitious items, like the date (1/1/20, 1/2/20, 1/3/20, etc.).

But that's not a good idea. To save time, do the following:

- To begin the series, move the pointer to the lower-right area of the final cell — the fill handle on your screen.

- You'll see it change to a plus symbol (+), and you'll need to click and pick the cells you want to fill.

- You'll see that they're filling up wonderfully, following the pattern you started. You may use the same technique to go up a column or left/right in rows.

Are you waiting for a good alternative? It is possible to auto-fill without too much of a pattern. After selecting a cell or cells, move the fill handle to see a menu of possibilities. The more

data you enter at the start, the better your AutoFill options will be generated by the Fill Series tool.

How to Flash in Excel Sheets

We are familiar with the Flash Fill functionality, which allows us to fill columns based on the first column's statistical pattern. When the top row is a unique header row, this feature comes in handy. Start typing in the first column if the phone numbers are formatted as "2126083111," but you want them to display as "(212)-608-3111."

Excel identifies the pattern and shows what it thinks you want by the second cell. To use them, press "enter." Ts, for example, can handle names, dates, and numbers.

If the second cell does not give you an exact range, type anything else since the pattern may be difficult to discern. After you've reached the data tab, press the Flash Fill button.

How to Paste Special with Formulas in Excel Sheet

Now consider a case where you have many decimal numbers that you wish to express as a percentage. The problem is that Numeral 1 should not be 100 percent. Excel will give you that option if you press the Percent Style button (Ctrl+Shift+ percent).

You want 1 to equal 1%, and to do so, you must divide it by 100. Paste Special underlines its significance at the moment.

- First, input and copy the number 100, then select all of the numbers you wish to convert.

- Select Paste Special and select "Divide" from the dropdown menu.

- All numbers will be converted to percentages.

Certainly, the same method may be used to swiftly multiply, add, or subtract integers.

Use filters to simplify your data

You don't have to check every single row just on the sheet at the same time while looking at really huge data sets. Instead, you choose to concentrate on data that meet precise criteria at specified times. That's where filters come in handy.

The purpose of filters is to help you limit your data and focus on only a few rows at a time. In Excel, you can apply a filter to any column. You may also choose which cells you wish to see at a certain time.

To add a filter, go to the Data tab and click "Filter." Next to your column heading will be an arrow that you must click. You may now choose between ascending and descending as your

preferred method of data organization. Aside from that, you may choose which rows you wish to display.

9.4 4 Super Cool Excel Tips and Tricks For Semi-Advanced

So, you're no longer an intermediate and know a few clever Excel tips and techniques that will surprise your coworkers. You can't call yourself a pro just yet because there's still a lot to learn. So, before you go out and get a job that involves Excel sheets, let's make you flawless.

Using Pivot Tables: Recognize and make sense of data

Pivot Tables may be used to restructure data in a spreadsheet. They don't change your data; nevertheless, they can compare different data in your spreadsheets and add it up if that's what you want.

Go to data> Pivot Table to create a Pivot Table. Excel will populate your Pivot Table for you. You can rearrange the order of your data.

- Report Filter: This feature allows you to focus on only a subset of the dataset's rows.

- Column Labels: These might be the headings of your dataset.

- Row Labels: These might be the rows in your dataset. Data from your column can be carried by both Columns and Rows labels.

- Value: The Value section allows you to take a different approach to your data. Rather than merely bringing in any number figure, you can total, average, count, and use your data.

How To Hide A Whole Sheet

There might be several worksheets in the file you're working on (each sheet is identified by a tab at the bottom, which you can name). The usual Excel worksheet of a semi-advanced user looks like this.

Rather than erasing it, you may conceal it, making its data available for reference and formulae on different pages in your worksheet.

- Select "Hide" after right-clicking the bottom sheet tab.
- Go to the View button at the top to find it again.
- A list will appear once you tap Unhide.
- Choose a name for your sheet, and that's all there is.

On the View tab menu at the top, there is also a Hide button. The entire worksheet you're using will be hidden when you press it. Although it seems that you have closed the file, Excel continues to operate.

When you exit the software, it asks whether you want to preserve all changes to the hidden Workbook. Furthermore, when you open the file, Excel presents you with what seems to be a blank worksheet until you hit Unhide again.

How to Utilize Personal Worksheet in MS Excel Sheet for Macros

You could find a workbook listed after unhiding a workbook — the Personal.XLSB file is the personal Workbook Excel created for you. Excel will open as a hidden workbook whenever you open it. So, what exactly is the point of using it? It's Macros, guys. A macro is associated with the worksheet in which it was produced. It means that it won't function on every single spreadsheet you've created by default (the way it does in word).

Do you wish to mark the presence of macros in all of your spreadsheet files? You must always keep the macro in Personal.XLSB. Select "Personal Macro Workbook" in the "Store macro in" section while recording the macro. To record a macro,

first, switch on the Developers tab, then go to the "File tab," click "Options," touch "Customize Ribbon," check "Developers" in the Main Tabs box, and then click "OK."

How to authenticate data to make Dropdowns

Are you excited to make a spreadsheet for your coworkers/employees to use? Creating a dropdown menu for options in certain cells is a straightforward task.

- After highlighting the "Data" tab, go to the Data tab and press Data Validation.

- After highlighting the cell, go to the Data tab and choose "List" from the "Allow:" dropdown menu.

- Then, in the "Source:" column, create a list with commas between the alternatives. You may also use the button next to the Source box to return to the same sheet and select a specific data series. It's the ideal method for dealing with long lists.

Even if you subsequently conceal the data, it will still work. Data Validation is a great approach to control/restrict data entry — for example, supply a date range, and people won't be able to enter dates before or after that range. You may also create the error message that they will see.

9.5 4 Super Cool Excel Tips and Tricks For Pro

Even if you're an expert, you haven't explored all of the Cool Excel Tricks and Tips available, so Excel sheets have such a lot to offer. Confidently you're not familiar with some formulas, and it's conceivable you're taking "shortcuts" on some duties. Everything comes to a head here. The following Excel tips can help you sharpen your thinking to the next level.

Use conditional Formatting: Creating cells necessarily alters color as per data

Conditional formatting is an important aspect of current Excel Tricks and Tips, and by utilizing it, you may make your data appear easier.

Conditional formatting allows you to modify the color of any cell based on the data it contains. So, for example, if you want to highlight certain values above average or in the top 10% of your spreadsheet's data, you may do so easily.

Using Excel to color code similarities across different rows is also feasible. You may quickly and easily see any information you think is essential at a given time using this method.

- First, choose the cells in the group that you want to perform conditional formatting on.

- Select "Conditional Formatting" from the dropdown menu on the Home menu.

- A popped-up box will offer more information about your formatting rule (if you want something unique, create your own rule)

- After you've finished, tap "OK." The findings will begin to show on their own.

The benefit of using dollar signs to keep a cell's formula similar no matter where it moves

You may have noticed a dollar symbol in certain Excel calculations if you've progressed to the semi-advanced and pro level. However, when we use it in a calculation, it does not represent an American dollar; few people know this. Instead, it confirms that the same rows and columns are kept the same no matter how many times the identical formula is derivative in adjacent rows.

A cell reference is relative, such as when you touch cell A5 from cell C5. You're pointing to a cell in the parallel row that's five columns to the left of the cell you're pointing at (5). That is what we refer to as the relative formula. It will change the formula's values depending on where it is moved when dealing with a relative formula from one cell to another.

However, there are occasions when we prefer that those values remain constant regardless of whether they are moved or not. We must convert the cell's formula into an absolute formula. If you wish to convert the relative formula (=A5+C5) to an absolute formula, add dollar signs to the column and row values, such as (=$A$5+$C$5). Wasn't that easy?

Use the VLOOKUP function to pull data from the sheet's one area to another.

You have two independent data sets on two separate spreadsheets that you want to integrate into a single spreadsheet. That might be a general necessity for semi-advanced & pro-people.

For example, in one spreadsheet, you have a list of your clients' names and phone numbers, while in the other, you have a list of these same clients' contact numbers and their separate business names. You'd want to have all of those people's names, phone numbers, & company names in one spot. Many readers' jobs may now include this, and you may not have realized there was a great shortcut accessible before today. VLOOKUP is a good option in this situation.

Before applying the formula, make sure one column appears the same in both places. Filter your data to make sure the column you're using to combine your information is similar,

with no additional spaces, and then write the following formula: =VLOOKUP (lookup value, table array, column number, [range lookup]) =VLOOKUP (lookup value, table array, column number, [range lookup]) =VLOOKUP (lookup value, table array, column number

NTIF function: Ideal to make MS Excel count numbers or maybe words in any kind of cells

It's good to delegate that task rather than manually counting how many times a certain number or value occurs. As a result, whenever a number or word appears in any range of cells, Excel utilizes the COUNTIF function to determine the Home. Let's assume you are trying to determine however many instances the word "Alexander" appears in your data collection.

- Our formula containing variables from our example down there: =COUNTIF(range, criterion) =COUNTIF(D:D, "Alexander") =COUNTIF(D:D, "Alexander") =COUNTIF(D:

- In this formula, there are multiple variables:

- Range refers to the region that our applied formula should cover. Because we're only interested in one column, we write "D:D" to indicate that the first and last columns are both D. "B:D" would be used if we were looking at columns B and D.

- Criteria: This is any piece of text or amount of text that we want Excel to count. Use quote marks if you like your results to still be in text rather than a number.

If you put the COUNTIF formulation into any cell & click "Enter," the total number of times the word "Alexander" appears in the dataset will be shown.

Chapter 10:
FAQS

10.1 How To Use Microsoft Excel: FAQ

Almost every aspect is covered and all levels in the Excel Tips & Tricks guide, and now it's time to take care of some small issues that crop up frequently. Almost everything is analyzed, and the most frequently asked questions and offered immediate answers.

How to get to the bottom of the Excel sheet?

Ctrl + end is the easiest solution. On the other hand, some of us like to browse the sheet's bottom using the scroll bar (located on the right). Once you've reached the bottom, activate any cell in any column with your data, then press the Ctrl + up arrow to reach your last row's first non-blank cell.

How to copy data from an Excel sheet to another using formula?

Selecting formula-specific paste possibilities in the destination cells is accessible while copying formulae to another place.

To copy/paste a formula, do the following:

- First, select the cell containing the formula you want to copy and press COMMAND + C.

- Next, select the cell into which you'd want to put the formula you just copied.

- If your intended call is on another worksheet, you must navigate to that worksheet and click the cell you want.

- Press COMMAND + V to paste the formula with all of its formattings. Another alternative is to press the arrow adjacent to the Paste button.

- Tapping the arrow brings up a menu of options.

- The following are a few alternatives that we frequently use:

- Formulas — If you only want to paste the formula and not the formatting from the source cell.

- Formulas & Number Formatting — This section is only for pasting formulas and number formatting (percent format, currency format, etc.)

- Paste Formula, Number Formatting, Border, Font, Shading, & Font Size from (Keep Source Formatting). This option is pasting the formula, number formatting, border, font, shading, & font size from the original cell.

- Paste Values — This option allows you to paste only the result, omitting the formula.

How to print an Excel sheet in A4 size?

Here's a quick instruction (in only 5 steps) to help you identify the options for changing the worksheet's paper size.

- After you've opened Excel, go to the Page Layout tab at the bottom of the window.

- In the Page Setup area of the ribbon, press the Size button.

- Select A4 from the dropdown menu.

- Press Print or Ctrl + P to bring up the Print option when you go to the file.

- The paper size is chosen to be A4.

However, depending on the formatting you added to your worksheet earlier, it may not print neatly on this paper size. What are your plans? Simply go to the Print menu and select No Scaling. You may choose "Fit All Rows on One Page" or "Fit Sheet." That's the fastest and most straightforward technique to improve the way your worksheet data prints.

How to fit the Excel sheet on one page in word?

- After selecting a page layout, press the little Dialog Box Launcher in the bottom right corner.

- A dialogue window for Page Setup will display.

- Select the Page tab in the Page Setup dialogue box.

- Select "Fit to" from the Scaling menu.

- right-click => AutoFit => AutoFit to contents. You can also choose 1 x 1 (wide x tall) in "fit to boxes."

- At the bottom of the Page Setup dialogue box, hit OK.

How to copy an excel sheet into word?

Placing data from Excel into PowerPoint or Word was, say, three decades ago, a perplexing task in the world of Office Suites. Today, it's butter on toast, whether copying and pasting data cells or a full-sized chart into another software. It would be beneficial if you thought about it; it's a link-and-embed technique, which means that if you alter the data in your spreadsheet, the data in the PowerPoint PPT or Word DOC will change. So, to avoid this, make a visual out of it. The word's own Paste Special tool is available for this purpose. Go to the Home tab at the top, select the Copy menu, and then the Copy as Picture option to get it out of Excel. Then you may paste the graphic into any software you choose.

How to remove lines in an Excel sheet?

When you're in an Excel spreadsheet, gridlines are always visible. So, how do you get rid of lines from an Excel sheet? Take the following steps:

- Navigate to the Page Layout tab.
- In Gridlines, uncheck the View item in the Sheet Options group.
- Your Excel worksheet will now be free of gridlines.

When experimenting with the gridlines, there are a few things to keep in mind:

It's also possible to use the ALT + WVG keyboard shortcut (enter W V G while hosting the ALT key). If the gridlines are visible, you can erase them using this shortcut. Otherwise, they will be apparent.

When you claim you're eliminating the gridlines, you're implying you're erasing the entire worksheet. It is a setting that is unique to each worksheet. As a result, even if you remove the gridlines from one worksheet, gridlines will still display on the others.

The gridlines can easily be removed by applying a background fill to your worksheet's cells. If the gridlines are visible, you can use a fill color in that region. The gridlines are no longer visible, and the fill color has taken its place. While filling in the whole worksheet with the fill color (You should remove the fill color to ensure the visibility of the gridlines).

How to insert an excel sheet into PowerPoint?

- On the Insert tab in PowerPoint, tap objects.

- In the Insert Object dialogue box, select Create from a file.

- Access the Browse box by tapping Browser. Locate the Excel worksheet containing the data you want to connect.

- Select Link and click OK before closing the Insert Object box.

Can I call things from one excel sheet to another?

Follow these procedures to have Excel insert any reference to another sheet:

- In the formula bar or the destination cell, begin entering a formula.

- Before you may add a reference to another worksheet, you must first switch the sheet.

- Next, choose the cell (or series of cells) you wish to refer to.

- When you've finished inputting your formula, press the Enter key to complete the operation.

> Is there a formula that can round a number to the nearest 5th increment or quarter increment?

=ROUND(A1/5,0)*5

=ROUND(A1/0.25,0)*0.25

> I'm seeking a formula that will examine a neighboring column, locate that value on another sheet, and return the data from that column?

=VLOOKUP(A2,Sheet2.A2: B100,FALSE)

> In A column, I'd want to include the 5 largest/smallest entries?

=SUM(LARGE(A:A,{1,2,3,4,5}))

> How do I choose 20 items at random from a list of 100?

- List the elements from A1 to A100.

- Enter the formula =RAND in B1:B100 ().

- Arrange the list by the B column, the top 20 rows are the ones you want.

- To get fresh B numbers, press F9.

- Make a new selection and repeat the process.

Is it feasible to sum visible cells alone with a SUMIF worksheet formula?

You can use the SUBTOTAL function with 9 as the first argument if the cells are hidden due to Auto Filtering.

I can use =SUMIF(A1:A20,">=10") to add all values greater than ten. But how can I combine two criteria by adding numbers between 5 & 10?

This is equivalent to the total of all >=5 minus the sum of all > 10:

=SUMIF(A1:A20,">=5")

-SUMIF(A1:A20,">10")

You may also use the following method:

=SUMPRODUCT((A1:A20>=5)

*(A1:A20<=10)*A1:A20)

Why does my function show #NAME?

The function may refer to an add-in functionality that isn't present in this Excel. Most of the time, it's an Analysis Tool Pak function; go to Tools > Add-Ins and make sure Analysis Tool Pak is checked.

Unlike Excel's built-in features, add-in functions do not automatically convert to regional language; hence American add-in features are inaccessible by default on a Norwegian machine and vice versa.

=CELL("Filename," A1) returns the full path to the file and the sheet name. Everything but the sheet name will be stripped away by

=MID(CELL("filename",A1),FIND("]",CELL("file-name",A1))+1,255). The formula will not operate unless the file is saved.

10.2 Calculation

- The formula is incorrectly calculated.

- The formula does not work at all.

- Instead of showing outcomes, formulas display them.

Is my formula incorrectly calculated?

There are 3 common causes for this type of message.

- The contents of the cells are not what they appear to be. A cell can display 1 (no decimals), including real or computed numbers of 0.6 or 1.4. You'll be startled if you add or multiply the number of those; Excel will compute using the actual cell contents, not the presented ones. Select "precision as presented" from the Tools > Options menu for a workaround, but make sure you understand what you're doing.

- A computer uses binary numbers, which has drawbacks. It is unable to accurately represent numbers such as 1/10. These numbers are rounded to the nearest 15 significant decimal digits, and Excel will be "off" around the 15th-16th digit. Some operations are affected, and some Boolean tests (those that look like 0.1=0.1) may return False. "Normal" work, such as sensible-number budgeting and everyday math, is typically unaffected, although this may not be the best tool for advanced science.

- You're utilizing the statistical capabilities in Excel. Some of them aren't up to par.

SLOPE(), INTERCEPT(), VAR(), STDEV(), LOGEST(), TREND(), FORECAST(), and other functions employ a numerically unstable method.

The spreadsheet does not calculate at all. Perhaps calculation is set to Manual. Alter this in Tools > Options menu.

Instead of the outcomes, the formulae are shown?

- Text formatting is an option for the cell. To alter it, go to format>Cells and select a category other than text on the Number tab, such as General or Number.

- The View Formulas option may be enabled. To disable it in Excel 2010, follow these steps:

- Select the Formulas tab from the Excel Ribbon. Click Show Formulas in the Formula Auditing group.

- Alternatively, in Excel 2003, go to Tools>Options. Remove the checkmark from Formulas on the View tab.

- Tip: Ctrl +' is the keyboard shortcut for displaying or hiding formulae.

10.3 Working with Tables and Lists

- Move data from the rows to the columns.

- Copy only the totals in data>Subtotals.

- The AutoFilter dropdown menu does not display all of the options.

- Separate the names of the first & last names.

- In a cell, create a dropdown menu.

Data stored in rows change to columns?

In Excel 2007 and later versions:

- Copy the data that you've selected.

- Choose the cell wherever you want the data to be pasted.

- On the Home tab of the ribbon, click paste, then Transpose.

In Excel 2003 and earlier versions:

- Copy the data that you've selected.

- Choose the cell wherever you want the data to be pasted.

- Select Edit>Paste Special from the menu bar.

- Select Transpose from the dropdown menu and click OK.

> I'd want to build a table that just contains these subtotals, not the hidden detail rows, using Data>Subtotals?

- Collapse the outline after applying the Subtotal so that only the row you wish to copy is visible.

- Pick the cells you want to work with.

- Select Edit>Go To and then the Special button.

- Click OK after selecting 'Visible Cells Only.'

- Select the Copy option.

- Transfer to a new sheet and paste.

> I don't see all things in the dropdown list when I use AutoFilter. What's to stop you?

An AutoFilter dropdown menu in previous versions of Excel will only show 1000 items. You might create a new column and divide the list into two or three groups using a formula, such as =IF(LEFT(C2,1)"N," "A-M," "N-Z")

Filter by these columns first and by the criteria you want to use. Another alternative is to select Custom from the dropdown menu and enter the criteria manually.

> How to divide a whole name into many cells?

Specify the comma (,) as a delimiter in data>Text to Columns.

> I'd want to make a cell such that the user may only select from a list of options, such as DHL, FedEx, or UPS?

Data Validation may be used to construct a dropdown list in a cell. You may input the options in the Source box to create a shortlist, as shown below.

- Choose data>Validation, then choose the cell(s) where you wish the list to display.

- Select the list from the Allow dropdown menu.

- Type "DHL, FEDEX, UPS" in the Source textbox (without the quotes)

10.4 Formatting

- Change the color of a cell dependent on the value in another cell.

- How do I make a cell flicker or flash?

- Place a bar over a character, for example, $\bar{X}$

> Is it possible to create a formula that accomplishes this: =IF(D25 does not match E25, then D25 font becomes red)?

- Choose cell D25.

- Select format>Conditional Formatting from the Format menu.

- Click on E25 on the worksheet to set Condition 1 - Cell Value Is Not Equal.

- Select the Font tab from the Format menu. Select Red from the Color dropdown menu.

- Click OK, OK.

No, instead, use conditional formatting to modify the color of the cell.

What is the best way to add a bar above a character?

- Adjust the size to Symbol before typing the character about which you want to get the overbar.

- Type the characters to make the bar (accent grave, may be above the Tab key)

- Next, type the character with the overbar in Symbol font or a different typeface. $\bar{X}$

Note: Some font sizes seem better on screen than others, but they should all look OK when printed.

10.5 International Issues

Translate Functions

These functions are in English and cannot be entered directly into Swedish Excel. Run the following macro:

```
Sub EnterEnglishFunction()
   ActiveCell.Formula = InputBox("English function:")
   End Sub
```

Paste the function in and click OK; it should translate in most situations.

How to use command and function shortcut keys?

Rather than using the mouse, utilize shortcut keys. Press the ALT key on the keyboard once in Word, Excel, or PowerPoint. Each tab of the ribbon should have a letter on it. The letter that corresponds to the ribbon tab should be pressed. A letter, letter combination, or number keystroke will now be shown for each function. They appear in capital letters, although they are not case-sensitive. If a series of letters appears, press the first one first, then the second.

Do Excel files open in previous versions of MS Office in "Read Only" mode?

Files open in "Read Only."

The consumer gets the following message while opening an Excel file: " "Although the file has already been converted to a format that you can work with, the following difficulties have arisen. The file has been opened in read-only mode to safeguard the original file. This worksheet has more rows and columns than this version of Excel can handle."

If a print area has been set, remove it. To see the sheets, use the Print Preview feature. Look for the number of pages in the lower-left corner. Hundreds of pages might be seen if grid lines, or colored sections were applied over an entire row or column. Only true data should include gridlines and colored regions. All additional extraneous formatting must be removed.

Without retyping everything, convert UPPERCASE into the lower or proper case?

Stop retyping and do these actions instead. It is a two-step procedure. First, construct a formula to transform the text, then copy-paste the values into a column.

168

- To the right of the column in question, add two blank columns (A). Column A is written in UPPERCASE, columns B and C are blank, and column D has a location.

- A formula would be entered in the first cell to the right of the first Name B2 in this example.

- Type the formula =Correct(A2) and hit enter to change the UPPERCASE NAME to the proper case name. The formula and the appropriate case name are shown in the example below.

- Now, click, hold, and drag the Autofill handle in the lower right-hand corner of B2 down the column to duplicate the formula that transforms the character case. Column A should not be deleted at this time.

- Now that column B shows the correct case, copy it and paste it into column C using Paste Special. Remember that Column B shows the calculation result, not the entire text. To pick a column, click on the column header B. Use CTRL+C or the copy icon to copy.

- Paste Special: Select Paste Special from the fast menu by right-clicking on cell C2. A dialogue window called Paste Special will open.

- Select Values from the dropdown menu. The value of the convert formula will be pasted into column C.

- If Column C appears to be right, remove Columns A and B.

Note: Two more formulae switch cases: =UPPER(cell) converts all characters to upper case. =LOWER(cell) converts all

characters to lower case. (cell) should be replaced with the actual cell location.

Selection Techniques

While working on an Excel document, you may utilize various selection strategies. Here are two that you may not be aware of.

The following is a huge block of text:

If the text you want to pick travels over the edge of your screen, or if clicking and dragging are too quickly, choose the first cell. Scroll to the final cell to be selected using the right scroll bar, then click while holding down the SHIFT key. Your option has just been highlighted.

Cells, rows, or columns that are not consecutive:

When choosing cells, rows, or columns, hold down the Control key.

Multiple Documents Opened

If you need to work with many documents simultaneously, Microsoft makes it simple to do so. There's a catch: all of these files have to be in the same folder. Select the files using the selection approaches, then click the Open button.

Choosing One File:

On the file, click once.

Selecting Consecutive Files:

Start with the first file and move your cursor to the final file. Click the last file while holding down the SHIFT key.

Selecting Non-Consecutive Files: Click on each file while holding down the CTRL key.

Column or Row Headings Must Be Visible

You can't see the column or row heads when a worksheet is bigger or longer than a screen view. You may need to use the column headers or row headings to input data correctly. Freeze Panes is the feature you require.

Freeze Panes are a feature in the Window grouping on the View ribbon. There are three alternatives available to you:

Freeze Top Row: This option maintains the top row displayed while scrolling down a document's rows.

Freeze First Column: This maintains the first column visible when scrolling straight across the columns in a document.

Freeze Panes: Both rows and columns are visible while scrolling through the content. You must first click below the needed row and one column to the right to freeze both rows and columns. Selecting cell B2 in this example will freeze row 1 and column A.

Leading Zero's dropped

If you wrote or imported data that starts with a zero, such as Security Numbers, Zip Codes, the beginning zero is removed from the column. Choose a cell, a column, or a row. Click the dialogue box launcher in the Numeric grouping from the Home Ribbon. Select Special from the category dropdown menu, then chooses the appropriate format.

Using Excel as a Data Source for Mail Merge

You can Mail Merge data from an Excel Spreadsheet into Word if Name and Address type entries are utilized. To utilize a spreadsheet for mail merge, the first row must include column headers, and the data must begin on the second row.

Linking Cells

Cells can all be linked on a single sheet, sheets, and Workbooks. Select the cell to be connected and duplicate it. Go to the relevant cell on that sheet, another sheet, or another workbook. Select Paste Special with a right-click on the cell. Click the Paste Link button in the Paste Special Dialog box. The copied linked cell reference looks like this within the same sheet: $11 =$B$11 (with absolute markers)

A reference to a pasted linked cell in a separate page of the same Workbook might look like this: =Sheet1. $11 B$ The Name of

the Workbook File would be $B$11, followed by the sheet name and then the cell position.

Can't Scroll in Excel? Here Are Reasons and Easy Fixes.

You can't scroll any longer in the Excel spreadsheet? Mainly scrolling up & down, but as well sideward doesn't work. There are really a number of likely reasons for that. Let us explore them below & let you scroll once again.

Purpose 1: Frozen panes may avoid you to scroll

Are there freeze panes? E.g. this first row or maybe column? If yes, attempt to unfreeze them. Consequently, go to View & tap on Freeze Panes & then again on Unfreeze Panes (if the icon shows "Freeze Panes" like when you scroll above it indicates that it is not the cause, and you must proceed to possible reason number 2 lower). Could you scroll now?

Purpose 2: A dialogue box or window is not closed

Are there any (secret) other windows / dialogue boxes wide open? For instance, a sort of window, although shown anywhere else (e.g. on any other screen)? In this case, the scrolling may be restricted as well.

Purpose 3: Holding down the Shift key stops scrolling

Are you pushing the Shift key? Perhaps something is pushing down on this key & you have not noticed it? In this case,

scrolling may not work. So, this solution here will be to just free the Shift button on this keyboard.

Buttons For Adding Images Or Charts In MS Excel Greyed Out?

Do you like to add a drawing, image, or charts to the Excel work-sheet, but the icons are dimmed out like the shown picture? There may be a simple answer to explain this.

Reason 1 for greyed out buttons: You are editing a cell

If you are typewriting in a cell or changing cell content, you could not insert charts or pictures. You initially have to "leave" this cell. Once you edit the cell (highlighted here) you could not insert & objects, such as images or charts. The icons are dimmed-out. Once you change a cell (highlighted here) you could not insert & objects, such as images or charts. The icons are dimmed out. So, how to "leave" the cell?

Simply tap somewhere in the workbook & press the "Esc" button (pushing the Esc key may be required if you change a function or formula – but please be sure that the edited formula must be saved). Has this resolved the issue? If not, go on with reason number two below.

Reason 2: Objects are hidden

Images, drawings or charts etc. missing. Select "For objects, display all" within the MS Excel choices.

Within the MS Excel settings, you could select if objects (including charts & images) shall be shown in the worksheet. If the setting is set to disappear all objects, you could not add any new items so that the icons are dimmed-out.

The setting is called "For objects, display:" Here you could select if you need to display all objects, including pictures, charts, dropdown lists & so on. Objects are in all-purpose everything that is not in the cells.

- Go to File & click on Options.

- On the left-hand side tap on "Advanced."

- Scroll down to the "Display choices for this worksheet:" The final bullet point shows, "For objects, showing:." Set a tick at "All."

Now the buttons shouldn't be greyed out any longer.

Reason 3: Worksheet Is protected

Sheet protection might prevent users from inserting images. Another cause is when the spreadsheet is protected. Varying on the sets of the sheet protection, you may not be permitted to

edit objects. The solution (or course): Unprotect the sheet. In order to do this, go to the Review ribbon and click on "Unprotect Sheet." It's possible that you have to enter a password, though.

Sheet Tabs in Excel Missing? How to Get Them Back.

Does the MS Excel file look a little like this? The names of the sheet at the end of the Excel window are lost. But no trouble, you could simply get them back. Certainly, the choice is a little bit secret. So, let's find out how to fix the sheet tabs.

Fix the sheet icons at the end of the Excel window to fix the tab names, only follow these quick steps:

Display the sheet icons: Go to the File, Options & mark the tick of "display sheet tabs" in an advanced tab.

- Go to the File.

- Tap on Options at the left end corner.

- Now, the Excel Options should be open. Go to Advance in the pane on the left.

- Scroll down to the worksheet choices. There is a tiny check-mark at "Showing sheet tabs." Be sure to set this checkmark & click on OK. That is it, the workbook names must be revealed now.

Why hide the tab names?

Well, here is one obvious motive: You like to make the MS Excel file look specialized, particularly when sharing the screen. Particularly with "messy," big MS Excel files it can make logic to not display them. Likewise, you have additional space on the window.

Something disappeared in Excel.

The following inquiries are about lost items, menus or icons in MS Excel. For most of them you can get back with either one of the two ways:

Check the View ribbon in Excel. There are some simple settings about the Excel window. If you cannot find it in the View ribbon, go to the Excel Options:

Click on "File," then on Options.

Go to the Advanced Tab on the left.

Scroll down, for example to workbook settings.

There are several annoyances & troubles in MS Excel. Most of them you could easily fix. For example: You can't scroll up and down. Or a formula bar is not here. Or you cannot group & ungroup rows & columns. The issue: Often it is not very instinctive to locate the right icon or setting.

Conclusion

Confidently, after reading this paperback, you will have realized that this paperback is superb for starting your journey with MS Excel and begin making your worksheets. This paperback includes various approaches and techniques to deal with MS Excel and begin guiding other persons who are a novice and new to Microsoft Excel.

Excel is a simple application program and knowing the tenets will assist learners and professionals get forward with their occupations. Novices must be more surprised with straightforward functionality such as rows, columns, and tables & could be less experienced with the software's improved features. In order to function the application in day-to-day workplace opportunities, you must have clear information about the software and its rewards.

A detailed Introduction to Microsoft Excel, its interface, Microsoft Excel cheat sheet, cell referencing in Excel, Basic and advanced formulae, conditional formatting, charts, tables, pivot tables and Excel tips, tricks, and FAQS with methods and practices. After reading all these topics, you will likely be going to make your or someone's life an easy place. It will probably improve your skills, deal with Excel problems, and even guide other people in everyday life. This book contains almost all the

aspects of MS Excel 2021 and enables you to become a skilled Excel specialist.

The key advantage of MS Excel is that it presents rapid data entry. As related to other data entry & analysis techniques, Excel has a Ribbon interface, which is a sequence of commands that could be used to perform particular tasks. The ribbon is made up of numerous tabs, and each one contains a number of command groups & their related keys. By selecting the appropriate tab, you could easily pick commands & carry out operations.

Generally, MS Excel facilitates you to manipulate, examine, and understand data, which will assist you in making healthier decisions & saving resources. MS Excel offers you the resources you ought to accomplish most of the tasks, whether you are using it for business or to manage private databases and expenditures. It is a valuable platform for creating customized template-based worksheets for commercial use, data analysis, and multimedia data management.

Printed in Great Britain
by Amazon

82554850R00108